MIRACLES

Theology
The Pilgrim's Regress
The Problem of Pain
The Screwtape Letters
The Case for Christianity
Christian Behaviour
Beyond Personality
The Great Divorce

Social Theory
The Abolition of Man

Literary Criticism
The Allegory of Love
Rehabilitations
The Personal Heresy
(in collaboration with W. M. Tillyard)
Preface to "Paradise Lost"
English Literature in the XVIth Century

Fiction
Out of the Silent Planet
Perelandra
That Hideous Strength
Till We Have Faces

For Children
The Chronicles of Narnia
1. The Magician's Nephew
2. The Lion, the Witch, and the Wardrobe
3. Prince Caspian
4. The Voyage of the Dawn Treader
5. The Silver Chair
6. The Horse and His Boy
7. The Last Battle

C. S. LEWIS

Fellow of Magdalene College, Cambridge

abridges his famous

MIRACLES:

a preliminary study

ASSOCIATION PRESS • New York

MIRACLES

This is an abridgment, approved and corrected by me, of a book which appeared more than ten years ago under the same title and is still available. I am satisfied that this abridgment preserves without distortion or falsification as much of the original as will fit into a paperback edition.

C.S.L.

This Reflection Book is published by

ASSOCIATION PRESS

291 Broadway, New York 7, N.Y.

Library of Congress catalog card number: 58-11529

To

CECIL AND DAPHNE HARWOOD

Among the hills a meteorite
Lies huge; and moss has overgrown,
And wind and rain with touches light
Made soft, the contours of the stone.

Thus easily can Earth digest
A cinder of sidereal fire,
And make her translunary guest
The native of an English shire.

Nor is it strange these wanderers
Find in her lap their fitting place,
For every particle that's hers
Came at the first from outer space.

All that is Earth has once been sky;
Down from the sun of old she came,
Or from some star that travelled by
Too close to his entangling flame.

Hence, if belated drops yet fall
From heaven, on these her plastic power
Still works as once it worked on all
The glad rush of the golden shower.

C.S.L.

(Reprinted by permission of *Time and Tide*)

Contents

I. *The Scope of This Book*

Those who wish to succeed must ask the right preliminary questions.

ARISTOTLE, *Metaphysics*, II, (III), i

In all my life I have met only one person who claims to have seen a ghost. And the interesting thing about the story is that that person disbelieved in the immortal soul before she saw the ghost and still disbelieves after seeing it. She says that what she saw must have been an illusion or a trick of the nerves. And obviously she may be right. Seeing is not believing.

For this reason, the question whether miracles occur can never be answered simply by experience. Every event which might claim to be a miracle is, in the last resort, something presented to our senses, something seen, heard, touched, smelled, or tasted. And our senses are not infallible. If anything extraordinary seems to have happened, we can always say that we have been the victims of an illusion. If we hold a philosophy which excludes the supernatural, this is what we always shall say. What we learn from experience depends on the kind of philosophy we bring to experience. It is therefore useless to appeal

9

to experience before we have settled, as well as we can, the philosophical question.

If immediate experience cannot prove or disprove the miraculous, still less can history do so. Many people think one can decide whether a miracle occurred in the past by examining the evidence "according to the ordinary rules of historical inquiry." But the ordinary rules cannot be worked until we have decided whether miracles are possible and, if so, how probable they are; for if they are impossible, then no amount of historical evidence will convince us. If they are possible but immensely improbable, then only mathematically demonstrative evidence will convince us: and since history never provides that degree of evidence for any event, history can never convince us that a miracle occurred. If, on the other hand, miracles are not intrinsically improbable, then the existing evidence will be sufficient to convince us that quite a number of miracles have occurred. The result of our historical inquiries thus depends on the philosophical views which we have been holding before we even began to look at the evidence. The philosophical question must therefore come first.

By *Nature* I mean the total system of interlocked events going on in this space-time continuum—interlocked so completely that you might call Nature not a system of events but a single, immensely complex, event. By *Naturalism* I mean the belief that Nature, so defined, is all that exists. Of course no Naturalist can admit miracles. To him, every particular event merely reflects, at a particular place and time, the going-on of the total system. Thus one argument against Naturalism is the difficulty, within it, of allowing the claims our own consciousness makes for itself. It claims that when we reason correctly our conclusion should be *logically dependent* on the steps of our argument. But the acts of thinking those steps were themselves events. If nothing but Nature exists they were then not *logically dependent* on, but *factually caused* by, the other events which preceded them (most of which were by the way nonrational). But logical dependence and factual causation are quite different and need not coincide: the thoughts of a mad or delirious man are as much caused as any others. It would therefore seem, in Naturalism, that every specimen of correct reasoning must depend on sheer luck: the order in which causation produced the thoughts (as natural events) just happened to coincide with the order which their logical dependence (as thoughts) demands. This is more than I can swallow.

If you believe in God you are not a Naturalist. You think that at least one thing (there might be more)* [1] exists besides Nature. God is neither the whole interlocking system, nor any item within it. He made it. He can unmake it. The question of miracles is the question whether He can, and would, also supple-

---

*All footnotes appear under "Notes by Chapters" at the end of the book.

ment or correct or interfere with it by feeding new events into the system He has made; events caused simply by Him, not by previous events inside the system, though, of course, once He has fed them in, they will then interlock with all subsequent events. This work deals only with the "can and would." I call it a "preliminary" study not because I mean to write another one on the subject but because it treats the question of possibility and propriety which is logically preliminary to the question whether God has actually done so. That is for the historians.

II. *A Chapter of Red Herrings*

Thence came forth Maul, a giant. This Maul did use to
spoil young Pilgrims with sophistry.

BUNYAN

From the admission that God exists and is the author
of Nature, it by no means follows that miracles must,
or even can, occur. God Himself might be a being of
such a kind that it was contrary to His character to
work miracles. Or again, He might have made Nature
the sort of thing that cannot be added to, subtracted
from, or modified. The case against Miracles accordingly relies on two different grounds. You think either
that the character of God excludes them or that the
character of Nature excludes them. We shall begin
with the second which is the more popular ground.
In this chapter I shall consider forms of it which are,
in my opinion, very superficial—which might even be
called misunderstandings or Red Herrings.

The first Red Herring is this. Any day you may
hear a man (and not necessarily a disbeliever in God)
say of some alleged miracle, "No. Of course I don't
believe that. We know it is contrary to the laws of
Nature. People could believe it in olden times because
they didn't know the laws of Nature. We know now
that it is a scientific impossibility."

By the "laws of Nature" such a man means, I think, the observed course of Nature. If he means anything more than that he is not the plain man I take him for but a philosophic Naturalist and will be dealt with in the next chapter. The man I have in view believes that mere experience (and specially those artificially contrived experiences which we call Experiments) can tell us what regularly happens in Nature. And he thinks that what we have discovered excludes the possibility of Miracle. This is a confusion of mind.

Granted that miracles *can* occur, it is, of course, for experience to say whether one has done so on any given occasion. But mere experience, even if prolonged for a million years, cannot tell us whether the thing is possible. Experiment finds out what regularly happens in Nature: the norm of rule to which she works. Those who believe in miracles are not denying that there is such a norm or rule: they are only saying that it can be suspended. A miracle is by definition an exception. How can the discovery of the rule tell you whether, granted a sufficient cause, the rule can be suspended? If we said that the rule was A, then experience might refute us by discovering that it was B. If we said that there was no rule, then experience might refute us by observing that there is. But we are saying neither of these things. We agree that there is a rule and that the rule is B. What has that got to do with the question whether the rule can be suspended? You reply, "But experience shows that it never has."

We reply, "Even if that were so, this would not prove that it never can. But does experience show that it never has? The world is full of stories of people who say they have experienced miracles. Perhaps the stories are false: perhaps they are true. But before you can decide on that historical question, you must first (as was pointed out in Chapter I) discover whether the thing is possible, and if possible, how probable."

The idea that the progress of science has somehow altered this question is closely bound up with the idea that people "in olden times" believed in miracles "because they didn't know the laws of Nature." Thus you will hear people say, "The early Christians believed that Christ was the son of a virgin, but we know that this is a scientific impossibility." Such people seem to have an idea that belief in miracles arose at a period when men were so ignorant of the course of Nature that they did not perceive a miracle to be contrary to it. A moment's thought shows this to be nonsense: and the story of the Virgin Birth is a particularly striking example. When St. Joseph discovered that his fiancée was going to have a baby, he not unnaturally decided to repudiate her. Why? Because he knew just as well as any modern gynecologist that in the ordinary course of Nature women do not have babies unless they have lain with men. No doubt the modern gynecologist knows several things about birth and begetting which St. Joseph did not know. But those things do not concern the main point—that a virgin birth is contrary to the course of Nature. And St. Joseph obviously knew *that*. In any sense in which it is true to say now, "The thing is scientifically impossible," he would have said the same: the thing always was, and was always known to be, impossible *unless* the regular processes of Nature were, in this particular case, being overruled or supplemented by something from beyond Nature.

When St. Joseph finally accepted the view that his fiancée's pregnancy was due not to unchastity but to a miracle, he accepted the miracle as something contrary to the known order of Nature. All records of miracles teach the same thing. In such stories the miracles excite fear and wonder (that is what the very word *miracle* implies) among the spectators, and are taken as evidence of supernatural power. If they were not known to be contrary to the laws of Nature how could they suggest the presence of the supernatural? How could they be surprising unless they were seen to be exceptions to the rules? And how can anything be seen to be an exception till the rules are known? If there ever were men who did not know the laws of Nature *at all,* they would have no idea of a miracle and feel no particular interest in one if it were performed before them. Nothing can seem extraordinary until you have discovered what is ordinary. Belief in miracles, far from depending on an ignorance of the laws of Nature, is only possible in so far as those laws are known. We have already seen that if you begin by ruling out the Supernatural you will perceive no miracles. We must now add that you will equally perceive no miracles until you believe that Nature works according to regular laws. If you have not yet noticed that the sun always rises in the East you will see nothing miraculous about its rising one morning in the West.

If the miracles were offered us as events that normally occurred, then the progress of science, whose business is to tell us what normally occurs, would render belief in them gradually harder and finally impossible. The progress of science has in just this way (and greatly to our benefit) made all sorts of things incredible which our ancestors believed; man-eating ants and gryphons in Scythia, men with one single gigantic foot, magnetic islands that draw all ships toward them, mermaids and fire-breathing dragons. But those things were never put forward as supernatural interruptions of the course of Nature. They were put forward as items within her ordinary course—in fact as "science." Later and better science has therefore rightly removed them. Miracles are in a wholly different position. If there were fire-breathing dragons our big-game hunters would find them: but no one ever pretended that the Virgin Birth or Christ's walking on the water could be reckoned on to recur. When a thing professes from the very outset to be a unique invasion of Nature by something from outside, increasing knowledge of Nature can never make it either more or less credible than it was at the beginning.

In this sense it is mere confusion of thought to suppose that advancing science has made it harder for us to accept miracles. We always knew they were contrary to the natural course of events; we know still that if there is something beyond Nature, they are possible. Those are the bare bones of the question; time and progress and science and civilization have not altered them in the least. The grounds for belief and disbelief are the same today as they were two thousand—or ten thousand—years ago. If St. Joseph had lacked faith to trust God or humility to perceive the holiness of his spouse, he could have disbelieved in the miraculous origin of her Son as easily as any modern man; and any modern man who believes in God can accept the miracle as easily as St. Joseph did. You and I may not agree, even by the end of this book, as to whether miracles happen or not. But at least let us not talk nonsense. Let us not allow vague rhetoric about the march of science to fool us into supposing that the most complicated account of birth, in terms of genes and spermatozoa, leaves us any more convinced than we were before that *Nature* does not send babies to young women who "know not a man."

The second Red Herring is this. Many people say, "They could believe in miracles in olden times because they had a false conception of the universe. They thought the Earth was the largest thing in it and Man the most important creature. It therefore seemed reasonable to suppose that the Creator was specially interested in Man and might even interrupt the course of Nature for his benefit. But now that we know the real immensity of the universe—now that we perceive our own planet and even the whole solar system to be only a speck—it becomes ludicrous to believe in them any longer. We have discovered our insignificance and can no longer suppose that God is so drastically concerned in our petty affairs."

Whatever its value may be as an argument, it may be stated at once that this view is quite wrong about facts. The immensity of the universe is not a recent discovery. More than seventeen hundred years ago Ptolemy taught that in relation to the distance of the fixed stars the whole Earth must be regarded as a point with no magnitude. His astronomical system was universally accepted in the Dark and Middle Ages. The insignificance of Earth was as much a commonplace to Boethius, King Alfred, Dane, and Chaucer as it was to H. G. Wells or Professor Haldane. Statements to the contrary in modern books are due to ignorance.

The real question is quite different from what we commonly suppose. The real question is why the spatial insignificance of Earth, after being asserted by Christian philosophers, sung by Christian poets, and commented on by Christian moralists for some fifteen centuries, without the slightest suspicion that it conflicted with their theology, should suddenly in quite modern times have been set up as a stock argument against Christianity and enjoyed, in that capacity, a brilliant career. I will offer a guess at the answer to this question presently. For the moment, let us consider the strength of this stock argument.

When the doctor at a post-mortem looks at the dead man's organs and diagnoses poison he has a clear idea of the different state in which the organs would have been if the man had died a natural death. If from the vastness of the universe and the smallness of Earth we diagnose that Christianity is false we ought to have a clear idea of the sort of universe we should have expected if it were true. But have we? Whatever space may really be, it is certain that our perceptions make it appear three-dimensional; and to a three-dimensional space no boundaries are conceivable. By the very forms of our perceptions therefore we must feel as if we lived somewhere in infinite space: and whatever size the Earth happens to be, it must of course be very small in comparison with infinity. And this infinite space must either be empty or contain bodies. If it were empty, or if it contained nothing but our own sun, then that vast vacancy would certainly be used as an argument against the very existence of God. Why, it would be asked, should He create one speck and leave all the rest of space to nonentity? If, on the other hand, we find (as we actually do) countless bodies floating in space, they must be either habitable or uninhabitable. Now the odd thing is that *both* alternatives are equally used as objections to Christianity.

If the universe is teeming with life other than ours, then this, we are told, makes it quite ridiculous to believe that God could be so concerned with the human race as to "come down from Heaven" and be made man for its redemption. If, on the other hand, our planet is really unique in harboring organic life, then this is thought to prove that life is only an accidental by-product in the universe and so again to disprove our religion. It seems that we are hard to please. We treat God as the police treat a man when he is arrested; whatever He does will be used in evidence against Him. This kind of objection to the Christian faith is not really based on the observed nature of the actual universe at all. You can make it without waiting to find out what the universe is like, for it will fit any kind of universe we choose to imagine. The doctor here can diagnose poison without looking at the corpse, for he has a theory of poison which he will maintain *whatever* the state of the organs turns out to be.

The reason that we cannot even imagine a universe so built as to exclude these objections is, perhaps, as follows. Man is a finite creature who has sense enough to know that he is finite: therefore, on any conceivable view, he finds himself dwarfed by reality as a whole. He is also a derivative being: the cause of his existence lies not in himself but (immediately) in his parents and (ultimately) *either* in the character of Nature as a whole or (if there is a God) in God. But there must be something, whether it be God or the totality of Nature, which exists in its own right or goes on "of its own accord": not as the product of causes beyond itself, but simply because it does. In the face of that something, whichever it turns out to be, man must feel his own derived existence to be unimportant, irrelevant, almost accidental.

There is no question of religious people fancying that all exists for man and scientific people discovering that it does not. Whether the ultimate and inexplicable being—that which simply is—turns out to be God or "the whole show," of course it does not exist for us. On either view we are faced with something which existed before the human race appeared and will exist after the Earth has become uninhabitable; which is utterly independent of us though we are totally dependent on it; and which, through vast ranges of its being, has no relevance to our own hopes and fears. For no man was, I suppose, ever so mad as to think that man, or all creation, *filled* the Divine Mind; if we are a small thing to space and time, space and time are a much smaller thing to God. It is a profound mistake to imagine that Christianity ever intended to dissipate the bewilderment and even the terror, the sense of our own nothingness, which come upon us when we think about the nature of things. It comes to intensify them. Without such sensations there is no religion. Many a man, brought up in the glib profession of some shallow form of Christianity, who comes through reading astronomy to realize for the first time how majestically indifferent reality is to man, and who perhaps abandons his religion on that account, may at that moment be having his first genuinely religious experience.

Christianity does not involve the belief that all things were made for man. It does involve the belief that God loves man and for his sake became man and died. I have not yet succeeded in seeing how what we know (and have known since the days of Ptolemy) about the size of the universe affects the credibility of this doctrine one way or the other.

The skeptic asks how we can believe that God so "came down" to this one tiny planet. The question would be embarrassing if we knew (1) that there are rational creatures on any of the other bodies that float in space; (2) that they have, like us, fallen and need redemption; (3) that their redemption must be in the same mode as ours; (4) that redemption in this mode has been withheld from them. But we know none of them. The universe may be full of happy lives that never needed redemption. It may be full of lives that have been redeemed in modes suitable to their condition, of which we can form no conception. It may be full of lives that have been redeemed in the very same mode as our own. It may be full of things quite other than life in which God is interested though we are not.

If it is maintained that anything so small as the Earth must, in any event, be too unimportant to merit the love of the Creator, we reply that no Christian ever supposed we did merit it. Christ did not die for men because they were intrinsically worth dying for, but because He is intrinsically love, and therefore loves infinitely. And what, after all, does the *size* of a world or a creature tell us about its "importance" or value?

There is no doubt that we all *feel* the incongruity of supposing, say, that the planet Earth might be more important than the Great Nebula in Andromeda. On the other hand, we are all equally certain that only a lunatic would think a man six-feet high necessarily more important than a man five-feet high, or a horse necessarily more important than a man, or a man's legs than his brain. In other words, this supposed ratio of size to importance feels plausible only when one of the sizes involved is very great. And that betrays the true basis of this type of thought. When a relation is perceived by reason, it is perceived to hold good universally. If our reason told us that size was proportional to importance, then small differences in size would be accompanied by small differences in importance just as surely as great differences in size were accompanied by great differences in importance. Your six-foot man would have to be slightly more valuable than the man of five feet, and your leg slightly more important than your brain—which everyone knows to be nonsense. The conclusion is inevitable: the importance we attach to great differences of size is an affair not of reason but of emotion—of that peculiar emotion which superiorities in size begin to produce in us only after a certain point of absolute size has been reached.

We are inveterate poets. When a quantity is very great we cease to regard it as a mere quantity. Our imaginations awake. Instead of mere quantity, we now have a quality—the Sublime. But for this, the merely arithmetical greatness of one of the millions of galaxies would be no more impressive than the figures in an account book. To a mind which did not share our emotions and lacked our imaginative energies, the argument against Christianity from the size of the universe would be simply unintelligible. It is therefore from ourselves that the material universe derives its power to overawe us. Men of sensibility look up on the night sky with awe: brutal and stupid men do not. When the silence of the eternal spaces terrified Pascal, it was Pascal's own greatness that enabled them to do so; to be frightened by the bigness of the nebulae is, almost literally, to be frightened at our own shadow; for light years and geological periods are mere arithmetic until the shadow of man, the poet, the maker of myths, falls upon them. As a Christian I do not say we are wrong to tremble at that shadow, for I believe it to be the shadow of an image of God. But if the vastness of Nature ever threatens to "o'ercrow" our spirits, we must remember that it is only Nature spiritualized by human imagination which does so.

This suggests a possible answer to the question raised a few pages ago—why the size of the universe, known for centuries, should first in modern times become an argument against Christianity. Has it perhaps done so because in modern times the imagination has become more sensitive to bigness? From this point of view the argument from size might almost be regarded as a by-product of the Romantic Movement in poetry. In addition to the absolute increase of imaginative vitality on this topic, there has pretty certainly been a decline on others. Any reader of old poetry can see that brightness appealed to ancient and medieval man more than bigness, and more than it does to us. Medieval thinkers believed that the stars must be somehow superior to the Earth because they looked bright and it did not. Moderns think that the galaxies ought to be more important than the Earth because they are bigger. Both states of mind can produce good poetry. Both can supply mental pictures which rouse very respectable emotions—emotions of awe, humility, or exhilaration. But taken as serious philosophical argument both are ridiculous. The atheist's argument from size is, in fact, an instance of just that picture thinking to which, as we shall see in a later chapter, the Christian is *not* committed. It is the particular mode in which picture thinking appears in the twentieth century; for what we fondly call "primitive" errors do not pass away. They merely change their form.

III. *Miracle and the Laws of Nature*

> It's a very odd thing—
> As odd as can be—
> That whatever Miss T. eats
> Turns into Miss T.
>
> W. DE LA MARE

Having cleared out of the way those objections which are based on a popular and confused notion that the "progress of science" has somehow made the world safe against Miracle, we must now consider the subject on a somewhat deeper level. The question is whether Nature can be known to be of such a kind that supernatural interferences with her are impossible. She is already known to be, in general, regular: she behaves according to fixed laws, many of which have been discovered, and which interlock with one another. There is, in this discussion, no question of mere failure or inaccuracy to keep these laws on the part of Nature, no question of chancey or spontaneous variation.[1] The only question is whether, granting the existence of a Power outside Nature, there is any intrinsic absurdity in the idea of its intervening to produce within Nature events which the regular "going on" of the whole natural system would never have produced.

28

Three conceptions of the "laws" of Nature have been held. (1) That they are mere brute facts, known only by observations, with no discoverable rhyme or reason about them. We know *that* Nature behaves thus and thus; we do not know why she does and can see no reason that she should not do the opposite. (2) That they are applications of the law of averages. The foundations of Nature are in the random and lawless. But the numbers of units we are dealing with are so enormous that the behavior of these crowds (like the behavior of very large masses of men) can be calculated with practical accuracy. What we call "impossible events" are events so overwhelmingly improbable—by actuarial standards—that we do not need to take them into account. (3) That the fundamental laws of physics are really what we call "necessary truths" like the truths of mathematics—in other words, that if we clearly understand what we are saying we shall see that the opposite would be meaningless nonsense. Thus it is a "law" that when one billiard ball shoves another the amount of momentum lost by the first ball must exactly equal the amount gained by the second. People who hold that the laws of Nature are necessary truths would say that all we have done is to split up the single event into two halves (adventures of ball A, and adventures of ball B) and then discover that "the two sides of the account balance." When we understand this we see that of course they *must* balance. The fundamental laws are in the long run merely statements that every event is itself and not some different event.

It will at once be clear that the first of these three theories gives no assurance against miracles—indeed no assurance that, even apart from miracles, the "laws" which we have hitherto observed will be obeyed tomorrow. If we have no notion why a thing happens, then of course we know no reason that it should not be otherwise, and therefore have no certainty that it might not some day be otherwise. The second theory, which depends on the law of averages, is in the same position. The assurance it gives us is of the same general kind as our assurance that a coin tossed a thousand times will not give the same result, say, nine hundred times: and that the longer you toss it the more nearly the numbers of Heads and Tails will come to being equal. But this is so only provided the coin is an honest coin. If it is a loaded coin our expectations may be disappointed. But the people who believe in miracles are maintaining precisely that the coin *is* loaded. The expectations based on the law of averages will work only for *undoctored* Nature. And the question whether miracles occur is just the question whether Nature is ever doctored.

The third view (that laws of Nature are necessary truths) seems at first sight to present an insurmountable obstacle to miracle. The breaking of them would, in that case, be a self-contradiction and not even Omnipotence can do what is self-contradictory. Therefore the laws cannot be broken. And therefore, shall we conclude, no miracle can ever occur?

We have gone too quickly. It is certain that the billiard balls will behave in a particular way, just as it is certain that if you divide a shilling unequally between two recipients, then A's share must exceed the half and B's share fall short of it by exactly the same amount. Provided, of course, that A does not by sleight of hand steal some of B's pennies at the very moment of the transaction. In the same way, you know what will happen to the two billiard balls—provided nothing interferes. If one ball encounters a roughness in the cloth which the other does not, their motion will not illustrate the law in the way you had expected. Of course what happens as a result of the roughness in the cloth will illustrate the law in some other way, but your original prediction will have been false. Or again, if I snatch up a cue and give one of the balls a little help, you will get a third result: and that third result will equally illustrate the laws of physics, and equally falsify your prediction. I shall have "spoiled the experiment." All interferences leave the law perfectly true. But every prediction of what will happen in a given instance is made under the proviso "other things being equal" or "if there are no interferences."

Whether other things *are* equal in a given case and whether interferences may occur is another matter. The arithmetician, as an arithmetician, does not know how likely A is to steal some of B's pennies when the shilling is being divided; you had better ask a criminologist. The physicist, as a physicist, does not know how likely I am to catch up a cue and "spoil" his experiment with the billiard balls: you had better ask someone who knows *me*. In the same way the physicist, as such, does not know how likely it is that some supernatural power is going to interfere with them: you had better ask a metaphysician. But the physicist does know, just because he is a physicist, that if the billiard balls are tampered with by any agency, natural or supernatural, which he had not taken into account, then their behavior must differ from what he expected —not because the law is false, but because it is true. The more certain we are of the law the more clearly we know that if new factors have been introduced the result will vary accordingly. What we do not know, as physicists, is whether supernatural power might be one of the new factors.

If the laws of Nature are necessary truths, no miracle can break them: but then no miracle needs to break them. It is with them as with the laws of arithmetic. If I put six pennies into a drawer on Monday and six more on Tuesday, the laws decree that— *other things being equal*—I shall find twelve pennies there on Wednesday. But if the drawer has been robbed I may in fact find only two. Something will have been broken (the lock of the drawer or the laws of England) but the laws of arithmetic will not have been broken. The new situation created by the thief will illustrate the laws of arithmetic just as well as the original situation. But if God comes to work miracles, He comes "like a thief in the night." Miracle is, from the point of view of the scientist, a form of doctoring, tampering, (if you like) cheating. It introduces a new factor into the situation, namely supernatural force, which the scientist had not reckoned on. He calculates what will happen, or what must have happened on a past occasion, in the belief that the situation, at that point of space and time, is or was A. But if supernatural force has been added, then the situation really is or was AB. And no one knows better than the scientist that AB *cannot* yield the same result as A. The necessary truth of the laws, far from making it impossible that miracles should occur, makes it certain that if the Supernatural is operating they must occur. For if the natural situation by itself, and the natural situation *plus* something else, yielded only the same result, it would be then that we should be faced with a lawless and unsystematic universe. The better you know that two and two make four, the better you know that two and three don't.

This perhaps helps to make a little clearer what the laws of Nature really are. We are in the habit of talking as if they caused events to happen; but they have never caused any event at all. The laws of motion do not set billiard balls moving: they analyze the motion after something else (say, a man with a cue, or a lurch of the liner, or, perhaps, supernatural power) has provided it. They produce no events: they state the pattern to which every event—if only it can be induced to happen—must conform, just as the rules of arithmetic state the pattern to which all transactions with money must conform—if only you can get hold of any money. Thus in one sense the laws of Nature cover the whole field of space and time; in another, what they leave out is precisely the whole real universe—the incessant torrent of actual events which make up true history. That must come from somewhere else. To think the laws can produce it is like thinking that you can create real money by simply doing sums. For every law, in the last resort, says, "If you have A, then you will get B." But first catch your A: the laws won't do it for you.

It is therefore inaccurate to define a miracle as something that breaks the laws of Nature. It doesn't. If I knock out my pipe I alter the position of a great many atoms: in the long run, and to an infinitesimal degree, of all the atoms there are. Nature digests or assimilates this event with perfect ease and harmonizes it in a twinkling with all other events. It is one more bit of raw material for the laws to apply to, and they apply. I have simply thrown one event into the general cataract of events and it finds itself at home there and conforms to all other events. If God annihilates or creates or deflects a unit of matter He has created a new situation at that point. Immediately all Nature domiciles this new situation, makes it at home in her realm, adapts all other events to it. It finds itself conforming to all the laws. If God creates a miraculous spermatozoon in the body of a virgin, it does not proceed to break any laws. The laws at once take it over. Nature is ready. Pregnancy follows, according to all the normal laws, and nine months later a child is born. We see every day that physical nature is not in the least incommoded by the daily inrush of events from biological nature or from psychological nature. If events ever come from beyond Nature altogether, she will be no more incommoded by them. Be sure she will rush to the point where she is invaded, as the defensive forces rush to a cut in our finger, and there hasten to accommodate the newcomer. The moment it enters her realm it obeys all her laws. Miraculous wine will intoxicate, miraculous conception will lead to pregnancy, inspired books will suffer all the ordinary processes of textual corruption, miraculous bread will be digested. The divine art of Miracle is not an art of suspending the pattern to which events conform but of feeding new events into that pattern. It does not violate the law's proviso, "If A, then B": it says, "But this time instead of A, A_2," and Nature, speaking through all her laws, replies, "Then B_2" and naturalizes the immigrant, as she well knows how. She is an accomplished hostess.

A miracle is emphatically not an event without cause or without results. Its cause is the activity of God: its results follow according to natural law. In the forward direction (that is, during the time which follows its occurrence) it is interlocked with all Nature just like any other event. Its peculiarity is that it is not in that way interlocked backward, interlocked with the previous history of Nature. And this is just what some people find intolerable. The reason they find it intolerable is that they start by taking Nature to be the whole of reality. And they are sure that all reality must be interrelated and consistent. I agree with them. But I think they have mistaken a partial system within reality, namely Nature, for the whole. That being so, the miracle and the previous history of Nature may be interlocked after all but not in the way the Naturalist expected: rather in a much more round-about fashion. The great complex event called Nature, and the new particular event introduced into it by the miracle, are related by their common origin in God, and doubtless, if we knew enough, most intricately related in His purpose and design, so that a Nature which had had a different history, and therefore been a different Nature, would have been invaded by different miracles or by none at all. In that way the miracle and the previous course of Nature are as well interlocked as any other two realities, but you must go back as far as their common Creator to find the interlocking. You will not find it *within* Nature.

The same sort of thing happens with any partial system. The behavior of fishes which are being studied in a tank makes a relatively closed system. Now suppose that the tank is shaken by a bomb in the neighborhood of the laboratory. The behavior of the fishes will now be no longer fully explicable by what was going on in the tank before the bomb fell: there will be a failure of backward interlocking. This does not mean that the bomb and the previous history of events within the tank are totally and finally unrelated. It does mean that to find their relation you must go back to the much larger reality which includes both the tank and the bomb—the reality of wartime England in which bombs are falling but some laboratories are still at work. You would never find it within the history of the tank. In the same way, the miracle is not *naturally* interlocked in the backward direction. To find how it is interlocked with the previous history of Nature you must replace both Nature and the miracle in a larger context. Everything *is* connected with everything else: but not all things are connected by the short and straight roads we expected.

The rightful demand that all reality should be consistent and systematic does not therefore exclude miracles: but it has a very valuable contribution to make to our conception of them. It reminds us that miracles, if they occur, must, like all other events, be revelations of the total harmony of all that exists. Nothing arbitrary, nothing simply "stuck on" and left unreconciled with the texture of total reality, can be admitted. By definition, miracles must of course interrupt the usual course of Nature; but if they are real they must, in the very act of so doing, assert all the more the unity and self-consistency of total reality at some deeper level. They will not be like unmetrical lumps of prose breaking the unity of a poem; they will be like the crowning metrical audacity which, though it may be paralleled nowhere else in the poem, yet, coming just where it does, and effecting just what it effects, is (to those who understand) the supreme revelation of the unity in the poet's conception. If what we call Nature is modified by supernatural power, then we may be sure that the capability of being so modified is of the essence of Nature—that the total event, if we could grasp it, would turn out to involve, by its very character, the possibility of such modifications. If Nature brings forth miracles then doubtless it is as "natural" for her to do so when impregnated by the masculine force beyond her as it is for a woman to bear children to a man. In calling them miracles we do not mean that they are contradictions or outrages; we mean that, left to her own resources, she could never produce them.

IV. *"Horrid Red Things"*

> We can call the attempt to refute theism by displaying
> the continuity of the belief in God with primitive delusion
> the method of anthropological intimidation.
>
> EDWYN BEVAN, *Symbolism and Belief,* chap. ii

I have argued that there is no security against Miracle
to be found by the study of Nature. She is not the
whole of reality but only a part; for all we know she
might be a small part. If that which is outside her
wishes to invade her she has, so far as we can see, no
defenses. But of course many who disbelieve in
Miracles would admit all this. Their objection comes
from the other side. They think that the Supernatural
would not invade: they accuse those who say that it
has done so of having a childish and unworthy notion
of the Supernatural. They therefore reject all forms of
Supernaturalism which assert such interferences and
invasions: and specially the form called Christianity,
for in it the miracles, or at least some miracles, are
more closely bound up with the fabric of the whole
belief than in any other. All the essentials of Hinduism
would, I think, remain unimpaired if you subtracted
the miraculous, and the same is almost true of Mo-
hammedanism. But you cannot do that with Christian-

ity. It is precisely the story of a great Miracle. A naturalistic Christianity leaves out all that is specifically Christian.

The difficulties of the unbeliever do not begin with questions about this or that particular miracle; they begin much further back. When a man who has had only the ordinary modern education looks into any authoritative statement of Christian doctrine, he finds himself face to face with what seems to him a wholly "savage" or "primitive" picture of the universe. He finds that God is supposed to have had a "Son," just as if God were a mythological deity like Jupiter or Odin. He finds that this "Son" is supposed to have "come down from Heaven," just as if God had a palace in the sky from which He had sent down His "Son" like a parachutist. He finds that this "Son" then "descended into Hell"—into some land of the dead under the surface of a (presumably) flat earth—and thence "ascended" again, as if by a balloon, into his Father's sky palace, where He finally sat down in a decorated chair placed a little to His Father's right. Everything seems to presuppose a conception of reality which the increase of our knowledge has been steadily refuting for the last two thousand years and which no honest man in his senses could return to today.

It is this impression which explains the contempt, and even disgust, felt by many people for the writings of modern Christians. When once a man is convinced that Christianity *in general* implies a local "Heaven," a flat earth, and a God who can have children, he naturally listens with impatience to our solutions of particular difficulties and our defenses against particular objections. The more ingenious we are in such solutions and defenses the more perverse we seem to him. "Of course," he says, "once the doctrines are there, clever people can invent clever arguments to defend them, just as, when once a historian has made a blunder he can go on inventing more and more elaborate theories to make it appear that it was not a blunder. But the real point is that none of these elaborate theories would have been thought of if he had read his documents correctly in the first instance. In the same way, is it not clear that Christian theology would never have come into existence at all if the writers of the New Testament had had the slightest knowledge of what the real universe is actually like?" Thus, at any rate, I used to think myself. The very man who taught me to think—a hard, satirical atheist (ex-Presbyterian) who doted on the *Golden Bough* and filled his house with the products of the Rationalist Press Association—thought in the same way; and he was a man as honest as the daylight, to whom I here willingly acknowledge an immense debt. His attitude to Christianity was for me the starting point of adult thinking; you may say it is bred in my bones. And yet, since those days, I have come to regard that attitude as a total misunderstanding.

Remembering, as I do, from within, the attitude of

the impatient skeptic, I realize very well how he is forearmed against anything I may say for the rest of this chapter. "I know exactly what this man is going to do," he murmurs. "He is going to start explaining all these mythological statements away. It is the invariable practice of these Christians. On any matter whereon science has not yet spoken and on which they cannot be checked, they will tell you some preposterous fairy tale. And then, the moment science makes a new advance and shows (as it invariably does) their statement to be untrue, they suddenly turn round and explain that they didn't mean what they said, that they were using a poetic metaphor or constructing an allegory, and that all they really intended was some harmless moral platitude. We are sick of this theological thimblerigging." Now I have a great deal of sympathy with that sickness and I freely admit that "modernist" Christianity has constantly played just the game of which the impatient skeptic accuses it. But I also think there is a kind of explaining which is not explaining away. In one sense I am going to do just what the skeptic thinks I am going to do: that is, I am going to distinguish what I regard as the "core" or "real meaning" of the doctrines from that in their expression which I regard as inessential and possibly even capable of being changed without damage. But then, what will drop away from the "real meaning" under my treatment will precisely *not* be the miraculous. It is the core itself, the core scraped as clean of inessentials as we can scrape it, which remains for me entirely miraculous, supernatural—nay, if you will, "primitive" and even "magical."

In order to explain this I must now touch on a subject which has an importance quite apart from our present purpose and of which everyone who wishes to think clearly should make himself master as soon as he possibly can. And he ought to begin by reading Owen Barfield's *Poetic Diction* and Edwyn Bevan's *Symbolism and Belief.* But for the present argument it will be enough to leave the deeper problems on one side and proceed in a "popular" and unambitious manner.

When I think about London I usually see a mental picture of Euston Station. But when I think (as I do) that London has several million inhabitants, I do not mean that there are several million images of people contained in my image of Euston Station. Nor do I mean that several millions of real people live in the real Euston Station. In fact, though I have the image while I am thinking about London, what I think or say is not *about* that image, and would be manifest nonsense if it were. It makes sense because it is not about my own mental pictures but about the real London, outside my imagination, of which no one can have an adequate mental picture at all. Or again, when we say that the sun is ninety-odd million miles away, we understand perfectly clearly what we mean by this number; we can divide and multiply it by other numbers and we can work out how long it would take to travel that distance at any given speed. But this clear *thinking* is accompanied by *imagining* which is ludicrously false to what we know that the reality must be.

To think, then, is one thing, and to imagine is another. What we think or say can be, and usually is, quite different from what we imagine or picture; and what we mean may be true when the mental images that accompany it are entirely false. It is, indeed, doubtful whether anyone except an extreme visualist, who is also a trained artist, ever has mental images which are particularly like the things he is thinking about.

In these examples the mental image is not only unlike the reality but is known to be unlike it, at least after a moment's reflection. I know that London is not merely Euston Station. Let us now go on to a slightly different predicament. I once heard a lady tell her young daughter that you would die if you ate too many tablets of aspirin. "But why?" asked the child, "it isn't poisonous." "How do you know it isn't poisonous?" said the mother. "Because," said the child, "when you crush an aspirin tablet you don't find horrid red things inside it." Clearly, when this child thought of poison she had a mental picture of Horrid Red Things, just as I have a picture of Euston when I think of London. The difference is that whereas I know my image to be very unlike the real London, the child thought that poison was *really* red.

To that extent she was mistaken. But this does not mean that everything she thought or said about poison was necessarily nonsensical. She knew perfectly well that a poison was something which killed you or made you ill if you swallowed it; and she knew, to some extent, which of the substances in her mother's house were poisonous. If a visitor to that house had been warned by the child, "Don't drink that. Mother says it is poison," he would have been ill advised to neglect the warning on the ground that "this child has a primitive idea of poison as Horrid Red Things, which my adult scientific knowledge has long since refuted."

We can now add to our previous statement (that thinking may be sound where the images that accompany it are false) the further statement: thinking may be sound in certain respects where it is accompanied not only by false images but by false images mistaken for true ones.

There is still a third situation to be dealt with. In our two previous examples we have been concerned with thought and imagination, but not with language. I had to picture Euston Station, but I did not need to *mention* it; the child thought that poison was Horrid Red Things, but she could talk about poison without saying so. But very often when we are talking about something which is not perceptible by the five senses we use words which, in one of their meanings, refer to things or actions that are. When a man says that he grasps an argument he is using a verb (*grasp*) which literally means to take something in the hands, but he is certainly not thinking that his mind has hands or that an argument can be seized like a gun. To avoid the word *grasp* he may change the form of expression and say, "I see your point," but he does not mean that a pointed object has appeared in his visual field. He may have a third shot and say, "I follow you," but he does not mean that he is walking behind you along a road. Everyone is familiar with this linguistic phenomenon, and the grammarians call it metaphor. But it is a serious mistake to think that metaphor is an optional thing which poets and orators may put into their work as a decoration and plain speakers can do without. The truth is that if we are going to talk at all about things which are not perceived by the senses, we are forced to use language metaphorically. Books on psychology or economics or politics are as continuously metaphorical as books of poetry or devotion. There is no other way of talking, as every philologist is aware. Those who wish can satisfy themselves on the point by reading the books I have already mentioned and the other books to which those two will lead them on. It is a study for a lifetime and I must here content myself with the mere statement; all speech about supersensibles is, and must be, metaphorical in the highest degree.

We have now three guiding principles before us. (1) That thought is distinct from the imagination which accompanies it. (2) That thought may be in the main sound even when the false images that accompany it are mistaken by the thinker for true ones. (3) That anyone who talks about things that cannot be seen, or touched, or heard, or the like, must inevitably talk *as if they could be* seen or touched or heard (for example, they talk of "complexes" and "repressions" *as if* desires could really be tied up in bundles or shoved back; of "growth" and "development" *as if* institutions could really grow like trees or unfold like flowers; of energy being "released" *as if* it were an animal let out of a cage).

Let us now apply this to the "savage" or "primitive" articles of the Christian creed. And let us admit at once that many Christians (though by no means all) when they make these assertions do have in mind just those crude mental pictures which so horrify the skeptic. When they say that Christ "came down from Heaven" they do have a vague image of something shooting or floating downward out of the sky. When they say that Christ is the "Son" of "the Father" they may have a picture of two human forms, the one looking rather older than the other. But we now know that the mere presence of these mental pictures does not, of itself, tell us anything about the reasonableness or absurdity of the thoughts they accompany. If absurd images meant absurd thought, then we should all be thinking nonsense all the time. And the Christians themselves make it clear that the images are not to be identified with the thing believed. They may picture the Father as a human form, but they also maintain that He has no body. They may picture Him older than the Son, but they also maintain that the one did not exist before the other, both having existed from all eternity. I am speaking, of course, about Christian adults. Christianity is not to be judged from the fancies of children any more than medicine from the ideas of the little girl who believed in Horrid Red Things.

At this stage I must turn aside to deal with a rather simple-minded illusion. When we point out that what the Christians mean is not to be identified with their mental pictures, some people say, "In that case, would it not be better to get rid of the mental pictures, and of the language which suggests them, altogether?" But this is impossible. The people who recommend it have not noticed that when they try to get rid of manlike or, as they are called, "anthropomorphic" images they merely succeed in substituting images of some other kind. "I don't believe in a personal God," says one, "but I do believe in a great spiritual force." What he has not noticed is that the word "force" has let in all sorts of images about winds and tides and electricity and gravitation. "I don't believe in a personal God," says another, "but I do believe we are all parts of one great Being which moves and works through us all"— not noticing that he has merely exchanged the image of a fatherly and royal-looking man for the image of some widely extended gas or fluid. A girl I knew was brought up by "higher thinking" parents to regard God as a perfect "substance"; in later life she realized that this had actually led her to think of Him as something like a vast tapioca pudding. (To make matters worse, she disliked tapioca.) We may feel ourselves quite safe from this degree of absurdity, but we are mistaken. If a man watches his own mind, I believe he will find that what profess to be specially advanced or philosophic conceptions of God are, in his thinking, always accompanied by vague images which, if inspected, would turn out to be even more absurd than the manlike images aroused by Christian theology; for man, after all, is the highest of the things we meet in sensuous experience. He has, at least, conquered the globe, honored (though not followed) virtue, achieved knowledge, made poetry, music, and art. If God exists at all it is not unreasonable to suppose that we are less unlike Him than anything else we know. No doubt we are unspeakably different from Him; to that extent all manlike images are false. But those images of shapeless mists and irrational forces which, unacknowledged, haunt the mind when we think we are rising to the conception of impersonal and absolute Being, must be very much more so. For images, of the one kind or of the other, will come; we cannot jump off our own shadow.

As far, then, as the adult Christian of modern times is concerned, the absurdity of the images does not imply absurdity in the doctrines; but it may be asked whether the early Christian was in the same position. Perhaps he mistook the images for true ones, and really believed in the sky palace or the decorated chair. But as we have seen from the example of the Horrid Red Things, even this would not necessarily invalidate everything that he thought on these subjects. The child in our example might know many truths about poison and even, in some particular cases, truths which a given adult might not know. We can suppose a Galilean peasant who thought that Christ had literally and physically "sat down at the right hand of the Father." If such a man had then gone to Alexandria and had a philosophical education he would have discovered that the Father had no right hand and did not sit on a throne. Is it conceivable that he would regard this as making any difference to what he had really intended, and valued, in the doctrine during the days of his naïveté? Unless we suppose him to have been not only a peasant but a fool (two very different things) physical details about a supposed celestial throne room would not have been what he cared about. What mattered must have been the belief that a person whom he had known as a man in Palestine had, as a person, survived death and was now operating as the supreme agent of the supernatural Being who governed and maintained the whole field of reality. And that belief would survive substantially unchanged after the falsity of the earlier images had been recognized.

Even if it could be shown, then, that the early

Christians accepted their imagery literally, this would
not mean that we are justified in relegating their
doctrines as a whole to the lumber room. Whether
they actually did, is another matter. The difficulty here
is that they were not writing as philosophers to satisfy
speculative curiosity about the nature of God and of
the universe. They *believed* in God; and once a man
does that, philosophical definiteness can never be the
first necessity. A drowning man does not analyze the
rope that is flung him, nor does an impassioned lover
consider the chemistry of his mistress's complexion.
Hence the sort of question we are now considering is
never raised by the New Testament writers. When
once it is raised, Christianity decides quite clearly that
the naïve images are false. The sect in the Egyptian
desert which thought that God was like a man is
condemned: the desert monk who felt he had lost
something by its correction is recognized as "muddle-
headed." [1] All three Persons of the Trinity are declared
"incomprehensible." [2] God is pronounced "inexpress-
ible, unthinkable, invisible to all created beings." [3]
The Second Person is not only bodiless but so unlike
man that if self-revelation had been His sole purpose
He would not have chosen to be incarnate in a human
form.[4] We do not find similar statements in the New
Testament, because the issue has not yet been made
explicit: but we do find statements which make it
certain how that issue will be decided when once it
becomes explicit. The title "Son" may sound "primi-

tive" and "naïve." But already in the New Testament
this "Son" is identified with the Discourse or Reason
or Word which was eternally "with God" and yet
also *was* God.[5] He is the all-pervasive principle of con-
cretion or cohesion whereby the universe holds together.[6] All things, and specially Life, arose *within*
Him,[7] and within Him all things will reach their
conclusion—the final statement of what they have been
trying to express.[8]

It is, of course, always possible to imagine an earlier
stratum of Christianity from which such ideas were
absent; just as it is always possible to say that anything
you dislike in Shakespeare was put in by an "adapter"
and the original play was free from it. But what have
such assumptions to do with serious inquiry? And here
the fabrication of them is specially perverse, since even
if we go back beyond Christianity into Judaism itself,
we shall not find the unambiguous anthropomorphism
(or manlikeness) we are looking for. Neither, I admit,
shall we find its denial. We shall find, on the one hand,
God pictured as living above "in the high and holy
place": we shall find, on the other, "Do not I fill
heaven and earth? saith the Lord."[9] We shall find
that in Ezekiel's vision God appeared (notice the
hesitating words) in "the likeness as the appearance of
a man."[10] But we shall find also the warning, "Take
ye therefore good heed unto yourselves. For ye saw
no manner of similitude on the day that the Lord
spake unto you in Horeb out of the midst of the fire—

lest ye corrupt yourselves and make a graven image."[11] Most baffling of all to a modern literalist, the God who seems to live locally in the sky, also *made* it.[12]

The reason that the modern literalist is puzzled is that he is trying to get out of the old writers something which is not there. Starting from a clear modern distinction between material and immaterial he tries to find out on which side of that distinction the ancient Hebrew conception fell. He forgets that the distinction itself has been made clear only by later thought.

We are often told that primitive man could not conceive pure spirit; but then neither could he conceive mere matter. A throne and a local habitation are attributed to God only at that stage when it is still impossible to regard the throne, or palace even, of an earthly king as merely physical objects. In earthly thrones and palaces it was the spiritual significance— as we should say, the "atmosphere"—that mattered to the ancient mind. As soon as the contrast of "spiritual" and "material" was before their minds, they knew God to be "spiritual" and realized that their religion had implied this all along. But at an earlier stage that contrast was not there. To regard that earlier stage as unspiritual because we find there no clear assertion of unembodied spirit, is a real misunderstanding. You might just as well call it spiritual because it contained no clear consciousness of mere matter. Mr. Barfield has shown, as regards the history of language, that words did not start by referring merely to physical objects and then get extended by metaphor to refer to emotions, mental states, and the like. On the contrary, what we now call the "literal and metaphorical" meanings have both been disengaged by analysis from an ancient unity of meaning which was neither or both. In the same way it is quite erroneous to think that man started with a "material" God or "Heaven" and gradually spiritualized them. He could not have started with something "material," for the "material," as we understand it, comes to be realized only by contrast to the "immaterial," and the two sides of the contrast grow at the same speed. He started with something which was neither and both. As long as we are trying to read back into that ancient unity either the one or the other of the two opposites which have since been analyzed out of it, we shall misread all early literature and ignore many states of consciousness which we ourselves still from time to time experience. The point is crucial not only for the present discussion but for any sound literary criticism or philosophy.

The Christian doctrines, and even the Jewish doctrines which preceded them, have always been statements about spiritual reality, not specimens of primitive physical science. Whatever is positive in the conception of the spiritual has always been contained in them; it is only its negative aspect (immateriality) which has had to wait for recognition until abstract thought was fully developed. The material imagery has never been taken literally by anyone who had reached the stage when he could understand what "taking it literally" meant. And now we come to the difference between "explaining" and "explaining away." It shows itself in two ways.

(1) Some people when they say that a thing is meant "metaphorically" conclude from this that it is hardly meant at all. They rightly think that Christ spoke metaphorically when He told us to carry the cross: they wrongly conclude that carrying the cross means nothing more than leading a respectable life and subscribing moderately to charities. They reasonably think that "hell-fire" is a metaphor—and unwisely conclude that it means nothing more serious than remorse. They say that the story of the Fall in Genesis is not literal; and then go on to say (I have heard them myself) that it was really a fall upward—which is like saying that because "My heart is broken" contains a metaphor, it therefore means "I feel very cheerful." This mode of interpretation I regard, frankly, as nonsense.

For me the Christian doctrines which are "metaphorical"—or which have become metaphorical with the increase of abstract thought—mean something which is just as "supernatural" or shocking after we have removed the ancient imagery as it was before. They mean that in addition to the physical or psychophysical universe known to the sciences, there exists an uncreated and unconditioned reality which causes the universe to be; that this reality has a positive structure or constitution which is usefully, though doubtless not completely, described in the doctrine of the Trinity; and that this reality, at a definite point in time, entered the universe we know by becoming one of its own creatures and there produced effects on the historical level which the normal workings of the natural universe do not produce; and that this has brought about a change in our relations to the unconditioned reality. It will be noticed that our colorless "entered the universe" is not a whit less metaphorical than the more picturesque "came down from Heaven." We have only substituted a picture of horizontal or unspecified movement for one of vertical movement. And every attempt to improve the ancient language will have the same result. These things not only cannot be asserted—they cannot even be presented for discussion—without metaphor. We can make our speech duller; we cannot make it more literal.

(2) These statements concern two things—the supernatural, unconditioned reality, and those events on the historical level which its irruption into the natural universe is held to have produced. The first thing is indescribable in "literal" speech, and therefore we rightly interpret all that is said about it metaphorically. But the second thing is in a wholly different position. Events on the historical level are the sort of things we can talk about literally. If they occurred, they were perceived by the senses of men. Legitimate "explanation" degenerates into muddled or dishonest "explaining away" as soon as we start applying to these events

the metaphorical interpretation which we rightly apply to the statements about God. The assertion that God has a Son was never intended to mean that He is a being propagating His kind by sexual intercourse: and so we do not alter Christianity by rendering explicit the fact that "sonship" is not used of Christ in exactly the same sense in which it is used of men. But the assertion that Jesus turned water into wine was meant perfectly literally, for this refers to something which, if it happened, was well within the reach of our senses and our language. When I say, "My heart is broken," you know perfectly well that I don't mean anything you could verify at a post-mortem. But when I say, "My bootlace is broken," then, if your own observation shows it to be intact, I am either lying or mistaken. The accounts of the "miracles" in first-century Palestine are either lies, or legends, or history. And if all, or the most important, of them are lies or legends, then the claim which Christianity has been making for the last two thousand years is simply false. No doubt it might even so contain noble sentiments and moral truths. So does Greek mythology; so does Norse. But that is quite a different affair.

Nothing in this chapter helps us to a decision about the probability or improbability of the Christian claim. We have merely removed a misunderstanding in order to secure for that question a fair hearing.

V. *The Propriety of Miracles*

The Principle at the same moment that it explains the
Rules supersedes them.

SEELEY, *Ecce Homo*, chap. XVI

Nature, then, offers us no security against miracles:
but perhaps one conception of God, current in much
popular religion of our own day, does. There are those
who accept God as a "great spiritual force" or "ultimate value" or "the indwelling principle of beauty,
goodness, and truth," but grow uneasy if you speak
of a God who has purposes, who acts and loves,
commands and forbids, and "worketh until now."
They feel it is too "anthropomorphic." Progress in
religion means for them stripping off the crude or
savage images; first the human shape, then human
passions, then activity, volition, personality—in the
end, every concrete or positive attribute. There is left
an inert and colorless abstraction. One sees how it
happens. Prophets and saints who have known God
deny these human attributes. But they do this to make
room for something positive, for the plenitude of love,
joy, and energy which they have encountered. We,
limping after, accept their negations but cannot replace
the things they eliminate with those vibrant realities
for whose sake alone they were eliminated. Thus at

every step "God" means less. We had better go back to images unless we can really go beyond them. The crudest Old Testament picture of Jahweh thundering, smiting, or "repenting"—even a Hindu idol with a hundred hands—is wiser in its naïveté than our abstraction. But we have a better image; the fierce, tender, consoling, exacting, ironic Christ, the most concrete Fact and most personal Person there ever was, is the image of the invisible God. We are reluctant to abandon an abstract Deity for this. No wonder. There comes a moment, in approaching a dimly seen object, when someone cries, "Look out! It's alive"; a moment when children who were pretending there were robbers in the house hush suddenly . . . was that a *real* footstep downstairs?

So here. It is a sort of Rubicon one goes across—or not. But if you do, you have no security against Miracle. You may be in for anything.

If the ultimate Fact is not an abstraction but the living God, then He might do things. He might work miracles. But would He? Many people of sincere piety feel that He would not. They think it unworthy of Him. It is petty and capricious tyrants who break their own laws: good and wise kings obey them. Only an incompetent workman will produce work which needs to be interfered with. This feeling springs from deep and noble sources in the mind and must always be treated with respect. Yet it is, I believe, founded on an error.

When schoolboys begin to be taught to make Latin verses at school they are very properly forbidden to have what is technically called "a spondee in the fifth foot." It is a good rule for boys because the normal hexameter does not have a spondee there: if boys were allowed to use this abnormal form they would be constantly doing it for convenience and might never get the typical music of the hexameter into their heads at all. But when the boys come to read Virgil they find that Virgil does the very thing they have been forbidden to do—not very often, but not so very rarely either. In the same way, young people who have just learned how to write English rhyming verse, may be shocked at finding "bad" rhymes (that is, half-rhymes) in the great poets. Even in carpentry or car driving or surgery there are, I expect, "licenses"—abnormal ways of doing things—which the master himself will use both safely and judiciously but which he would think it unwise to teach his pupils.

Now one often finds that the beginner, who has just mastered the strict formal rules, is overpunctilious and pedantic about them. And the mere critic, who is never going to begin himself, may be more pedantic still. The classical critics were shocked at the "irregularity" or "licenses" of Shakespeare. A stupid schoolboy might think that the abnormal hexameters in Virgil, or the half-rhymes in English poets, were due to incompetence. In reality, of course, every one of them is there for a purpose and breaks the superficial regularity of the meter in obedience to a higher and subtler law.

In other words, there are rules behind the rules, and a unity which is deeper than uniformity. A supreme workman will never break by one note or one syllable or one stroke of the brush the living and inward law of the work he is producing. But he will break without scruple any number of those superficial regularities and orthodoxies which little, unimaginative critics mistake for its laws. The extent to which one can distinguish a just "license" from a mere botch or failure of unity depends on the extent to which one has grasped the real and inward significance of the work as a whole. If we had grasped as a whole the innermost spirit of that "work which God worketh from the beginning to the end," and of which Nature is only a part and perhaps a small part, we should be in a position to decide whether miraculous interruptions of Nature's history were mere improprieties unworthy of the Great Workman or expressions of the truest and deepest unity in His total work. In fact, of course, we are in no such position.

Who can suppose that God's eternal act, seen from within, would be that same complexity of mathematical relations which Nature, scientifically studied, reveals? It is like thinking that a poet builds up his line out of those metrical feet into which we can analyze it, or that living speech takes grammar as its starting point.

How a miracle can be no inconsistency, but the

highest consistency, will be clear to those who have
read Miss Dorothy Sayers' indispensable book, *The
Mind of the Maker*. Miss Sayers' thesis is based on
the analogy between God's relation to the world, on
the one hand, and an author's relation to his book on
the other. If you are writing a story, miracles or abnormal events may be bad art, or they may not. If,
for example, you are writing an ordinary realistic novel
and have got your characters into a hopeless muddle,
it would be quite intolerable if you suddenly cut the
knot and secured a happy ending by having a fortune
left to the hero from an unexpected quarter.

On the other hand, there is nothing against taking
as your subject from the outset the adventures of a
man who inherits an unexpected fortune. The unusual
event is perfectly permissible if it is what you are
really writing *about*: it is an artistic crime if you
simply drag it in by the heels to get yourself out of a
hole. The ghost story is a legitimate form of art; but
you must not bring a ghost into an ordinary novel to
get over a difficulty in the plot. Now there is no doubt
that a great deal of the modern objection to miracles
is based on the suspicion that they are marvels of the
wrong sort; that a story of a certain kind (Nature) is
arbitrarily interfered with, to get the characters out
of a difficulty, by events that do not really belong to
that kind of story. Some people probably think of the
Resurrection as a desperate last-moment expedient to

save the Hero from a situation which had got out of the Author's control.

The reader may set his mind at rest. If I thought miracles were like that, I should not believe in them. If they have occurred, they have occurred because they are the very thing this universal story is about. They are not exceptions (however rarely they occur) nor irrelevancies. They are precisely those chapters in this great story on which the plot turns. Death and Resurrection are what the story is about; and, had we but eyes to see it, this has been hinted on every page, met us, in some disguise, at every turn, and even been muttered in conversations between such minor characters (if they are minor characters) as the vegetables. If you have hitherto disbelieved in miracles, it is worth pausing a moment to consider whether this is not chiefly because you thought you had discovered what the story was really about—that atoms, and time and space, and economics and politics were the main plot. And is it certain you were right? It is easy to make mistakes in such matters. A friend of mine wrote a play in which the main idea was that the hero had a pathological horror of trees and a mania for cutting them down. But naturally other things came in as well; there was some sort of love story mixed up with it. And the trees killed the man in the end. When my friend had written it, he sent it to an older man to criticize. It came back with the comment, "Not bad.

But I'd cut out those bits of *padding* about the trees."
To be sure, God might be expected to make a better
story than my friend. But it is a very *long* story, with
a complicated plot; and we are not, perhaps, very
attentive readers.

VI. *On Probability*

Probability is founded on the presumption of a resemblance
between those objects of which we have had experience and
those of which we have had none; and therefore it is
impossible that this presumption can arise from probability.
                    DAVID HUME, *Treatise of Human Nature*, I, III, vi

The argument up to date shows that miracles are
possible and that there is nothing antecedently ridiculous in the stories which say that God has sometimes
performed them. This does not mean, of course, that
we are committed to believing all stories of miracles.
Most stories about miraculous events are probably
false: if it comes to that, most stories about natural
events are false. Lies, exaggerations, misunderstandings, and hearsay make up perhaps more than half
of all that is said and written in the world. We must
therefore find a criterion whereby to judge any
particular story of the miraculous.

In one sense, of course, our criterion is plain. Those
stories are to be accepted for which the historical
evidence is sufficiently good. But then, as we saw at
the outset, the answer to the question, "How much
evidence should we require for this story?" depends on
our answer to the question, "How far is this story

intrinsically probable?" We must therefore find a criterion of probability.

The ordinary procedure of the modern historian, even if he admits the possibility of Miracle, is to admit no particular instance of it until every possibility of "natural" explanation has been tried and failed. That is, he will accept the most improbable "natural" explanations rather than say that a miracle occurred. Collective hallucination, hypnotism of unconsenting spectators, widespread instantaneous conspiracy in lying by persons not otherwise known to be liars and not likely to gain by the lie—all these are known to be very improbable events: so improbable that except for the special purpose of excluding a miracle, they are never suggested. But they are preferred to the admission of a miracle.

Such a procedure is, from the purely historical point of view, sheer midsummer madness *unless* we start by knowing that any miracle whatever is more improbable than the most improbable natural event. Do we know this?

We must distinguish the different kinds of improbability. Since miracles are, by definition, rarer than other events, it is obviously improbable beforehand that one will occur at any given place and time. In that sense every miracle is improbable. But that sort of improbability does not make incredible the story that a miracle *has* happened; for in the same sense all events whatever were once improbable. It is immensely improbable beforehand that a pebble dropped from the stratosphere over London will hit any given spot, or that any one particular person will win a large lottery. But the report that the pebble has landed outside such and such a shop or that Mr. So-and-So has won the lottery is not at all incredible. When you consider the immense number of meetings and fertile unions between ancestors which were necessary in order that you should be born, you perceive that it was once immensely improbable that such a person as you should come to exist: but once you are here, the report of your existence is not in the least incredible. With probability of this kind—antecedent probability of chances—we are not here concerned. Our business is with historical probability.

Ever since Hume's famous "Essay on Miracles" it has been believed that historical statements about miracles are the most intrinsically improbable of all historical statements. According to Hume, probability rests on what may be called the majority vote of our past experiences. The more often a thing has been known to happen, the more probable it is that it should happen again; and the less often the less probable. Now the regularity of Nature's course, says Hume, is supported by something better than the majority vote of past experiences: it is supported by their unanimous vote, or, as Hume says, by "firm and unalterable experience." There is, in fact, "uniform experience" against Miracle; otherwise, says Hume, it would not be Miracle. A miracle is therefore the most improbable of all events. It is always more probable that the witnesses were lying or mistaken than that a miracle occurred.

Now of course we must agree with Hume that if there is absolutely "uniform experience" against miracles, if in other words they have never happened, why then they never have. Unfortunately we know the experience against them to be uniform only if we know that all the reports of them are false. And we can know all the reports to be false only if we know already that miracles have never occurred. In fact, we are arguing in a circle.

There is also an objection to Hume which leads us deeper into our problem. The whole idea of probability (as Hume understands it) depends on the principle of the Uniformity of Nature. Unless Nature always goes on in the same way, the fact that a thing had happened ten million times would not make it a whit more probable that it would happen again. And how do we know the Uniformity of Nature? A moment's thought shows that we do not know it by experience. We observe many regularities in Nature. But of course all the observations that men have made or will make while the race lasts cover only a minute fraction of the events that actually go on. Our observations would therefore be of no use unless we felt sure that Nature when we are not watching her behaves in the same way as when we are: in other words, unless we be-

lieved in the Uniformity of Nature. Experience therefore cannot prove uniformity, because uniformity has
to be assumed before experience proves anything. And
mere length of experience does not help matters. It
is no good saying, "Each fresh experience confirms our
belief in uniformity and therefore we reasonably
expect that it will always be confirmed"; for that
argument works only on the assumption that the
future will resemble the past—which is simply the
assumption of uniformity under a new name. Can we
say that uniformity is at any rate very probable? Unfortunately not. We have just seen that all probabilities
depend on *it*. Unless Nature is uniform, nothing is
either probable or improbable. And clearly the assumption which you have to make before there is any such
thing as probability cannot itself be probable.

The odd thing is that no man knew this better than
Hume. His "Essay on Miracles" is quite inconsistent
with the more radical, and honorable, skepticism of his
main work.

Probabilities of the kind that Hume is concerned
with hold inside the framework of an assumed Uniformity of Nature. When the question of miracles is
raised we are asking about the validity or perfection
of the frame itself. No study of probabilities inside a
given frame can ever tell us how probable it is that
the frame itself can be violated. Granted a school
timetable with French on Tuesday mornings at ten
o'clock, it is really probable that Jones, who always

skimps his French preparation, will be in trouble next Tuesday, and that he was in trouble on any previous Tuesday. But what does this tell us about the probability of the timetable's being altered? To find that out you must eavesdrop in the masters' common-room. It is no use studying the timetable.

If we stick to Hume's method, far from getting what he hoped (namely, the conclusion that all miracles are infinitely improbable) we get a complete deadlock. The only kind of probability he allows holds exclusively within the frame of uniformity. When uniformity is itself in question (and it is in question the moment we ask whether miracles occur) this kind of probability is suspended. And Hume knows no other. By his method, therefore, we cannot say that uniformity is either probable or improbable; and equally we cannot say that miracles are either probable or improbable. We have impounded *both* uniformity *and* miracles in a sort of limbo where probability and improbability can never come. This result is equally disastrous for the scientist and the theologian; but along Hume's lines there is nothing whatever to be done about it.

Our only hope, then, will be to cast about for some quite different kind of probability. Let us for the moment cease to ask what right we have to believe in the Uniformity of Nature, and ask why in fact men do believe in it. I think the belief has three causes, two of which are irrational. In the first place, we are creatures of habit. We expect new situations to resemble old ones. It is a tendency which we share with animals; one can see it working, often to very comic results, in our dogs and cats. In the second place, when we plan our actions, we have to leave out of account the theoretical possibility that Nature might not behave as usual tomorrow, because we can do nothing about it. It is not worth bothering about because no action can be taken to meet it. And what we habitually put out of our minds we soon forget. The picture of uniformity thus comes to dominate our minds without rival and we believe it. Both these causes are irrational and would be just as effective in building up a false belief as in building up a true one.

But I am convinced that there is a third cause. "In science," said the late Sir Arthur Eddington, "we sometimes have convictions which we cherish but cannot justify; we are influenced by some innate sense of the fitness of things." This may sound a perilously subjective and aesthetic criterion; but can one doubt that it is a principal source of our belief in uniformity? A universe in which unprecedented and unpredictable events were at every moment flung into Nature would not merely be inconvenient to us: it would be profoundly repugnant. We will not accept such a universe on any terms whatever. It is utterly detestable to us. It shocks our "sense of the fitness of things." In advance of experience, in the teeth of many experiences, we are already enlisted on the side of uniformity, for of course science actually proceeds by concentrating not on the regularities of Nature but on her apparent irregularities. It is the apparent irregularity that prompts each new hypothesis. It does so because we refuse to acquiesce in irregularities: we never rest till we have formed and verified a hypothesis which enables us to say that they were not really irregularities at all. Nature as it comes to us looks at first like a mass of irregularities. The stove which lit all right yesterday won't light today; the water which was wholesome last year is poisonous this year. The whole mass of seemingly irregular experience could never have been turned into scientific knowledge at all unless from the very start we had brought to it a faith in uniformity which almost no number of disappointments can shake.

This faith—the preference—is it a thing we can trust? Or is it only the way our minds happen to work? It is useless to say that it has hitherto always been confirmed by the event. That is no good unless you (at least silently) add, "And therefore always will be": and you cannot add that unless you know already that our faith in uniformity is well grounded. And that is just what we are now asking. Does this sense of fitness of ours correspond to anything in external reality?

The answer depends on the metaphysic one holds. If all that exists is Nature, the great mindless interlocking event, if our own deepest convictions are merely the by-products of a nonrational process, then clearly there is not the slightest ground for supposing that our sense of fitness and our consequent faith in uniformity tell us anything about a reality external to ourselves. Our convictions are simply a fact *about us* —like the color of our hair. If Naturalism is true we have no reason to trust our conviction that Nature is uniform. It can be trusted only if quite a different metaphysic is true. If the deepest thing in reality, the Fact which is the source of all other facthood, is a thing in some degree like ourselves—if it is a Rational Spirit and we derive our rational spirituality from It—then indeed our conviction can be trusted. Our repugnance to disorder is derived from Nature's Creator and ours. The disorderly world which we cannot endure to believe in is the disorderly world He would not have endured to create. Our conviction that the timetable will not be perpetually or meaninglessly altered is sound because we have (in a sense) eavesdropped in the masters' common-room.

The sciences logically require a metaphysic of this sort. Our greatest natural philosopher thinks it is also the metaphysic out of which they originally grew. Professor Whitehead points out[1] that centuries of belief in a God who combined "the personal energy of Jehovah" with "the rationality of a Greek philosopher" first produced that firm expectation of systematic order which rendered possible the birth of modern science. Men became scientific because they expected law in

Nature, and they expected law in Nature because they believed in a Legislator. In most modern scientists this belief has died; it will be interesting to see how long their confidence in uniformity survives it. Two significant developments have already appeared—the hypothesis of a lawless subnature, and the surrender of the claim that science is true. We may be living nearer than we suppose to the end of the Scientific Age.

But if we admit God, must we admit Miracle? Indeed, indeed, you have no security against it. That is the bargain. Theology says to you in effect, "Admit God and with Him the risk of a few miracles, and I in return will ratify your faith in uniformity as regards the overwhelming majority of events." The philosophy which forbids you to make uniformity absolute is also the philosophy which offers you solid grounds for believing it to be general, to be *almost* absolute. The Being who threatens Nature's claim to omnipotence confirms her in her lawful occasions. Give us this ha'porth of tar and we will save the ship. The alternative is really much worse. Try to make Nature absolute, and you find that her uniformity is not even probable. By claiming too much, you get nothing. You get the deadlock, as in Hume. Theology offers you a working arrangement, which leaves the scientist free to continue his experiments and the Christian to continue his prayers.

We have also, I suggest, found what we were looking for—a criterion whereby to judge the intrinsic probability of an alleged miracle. We must judge it by our "innate sense of the fitness of things," that same sense of fitness which led us to anticipate that the universe would be orderly. I do not mean, of course, that we are to use this sense in deciding whether miracles in general are possible: we know that they are on philosophical grounds. Nor do I mean that a sense of fitness will do instead of close inquiry into the historical evidence. As I have repeatedly pointed out, the historical evidence cannot be estimated unless we have first estimated the intrinsic probability of the recorded event. It is in making that estimate as regards each story of the miraculous that our sense of fitness comes into play.

If in giving such weight to the sense of fitness I were doing anything new, I should feel rather nervous. In reality I am merely giving formal acknowledgment to a principle which is always used. Whatever men may *say,* no one really thinks that the Christian doctrine of the Resurrection is exactly on the same level with some pious tittle-tattle about how Mother Egarée Louise miraculously found her second-best thimble by the aid of St. Anthony. The religious and the irreligious are really quite agreed on the point. The whoop of delight with which the skeptic would unearth the story of the thimble, and the "rosy pudency" with which the Christian would keep it in the background, both tell the same tale. Even those who think all stories of miracles absurd think some very much more absurd than others: even those who believe them all (if anyone does) think that some require a specially robust faith. The criterion which both parties are actually using is that of fitness. More than half the disbelief in miracles that exist is based on a sense of their *unfitness*: a conviction (due, as I have argued, to false philosophy) that they are unsuitable to the dignity of God or Nature or else to the indignity and insignificance of man.

In the three following chapters I shall try to present the central miracles of the Christian Faith in such a way as to exhibit their "fitness." I shall not, however, proceed by formally setting out the conditions which "fitness" in the abstract ought to satisfy and then dovetailing the miracles into that scheme. Our "sense of fitness" is too delicate and elusive a thing to submit to such treatment. If I succeed, the fitness—and if I fail, the unfitness—of these miracles will of itself become apparent while we study them.

VII. *The Grand Miracle*

A light that shone from behind the sun; the sun was not
so fierce as to pierce where that light could.

CHARLES WILLIAMS

The central miracle asserted by Christians is the Incarnation. They say that God became Man. Every
other miracle prepares for this, or exhibits this, or
results from this. Just as every natural event is the
manifestation at a particular place and moment of
Nature's total character, so every particular Christian
miracle manifests at a particular place and moment
the character and significance of the Incarnation. There
is no question in Christianity of arbitrary interferences
just scattered about. It relates not a series of discon-
nected raids on Nature but the various steps of a
strategically coherent invasion—an invasion which
intends complete conquest and "occupation." The
fitness, and therefore credibility, of the particular
miracles depends on their relation to the Grand
Miracle; all discussion of them in isolation from it is
futile.

The fitness or credibility of the Grand Miracle itself
cannot, obviously, be judged by the same standard.
And let us admit at once that it is very difficult to

find a standard by which it can be judged. If the thing happened, it was the central event in the history of the Earth—the very thing that the whole story has been about. Since it happened only once, it is by Hume's standards infinitely improbable. But then the whole history of the Earth has also happened only once; is it therefore incredible? Hence the difficulty, which weighs upon Christian and atheist alike, of estimating the probability of the Incarnation. It is like asking whether the existence of Nature herself is intrinsically probable. That is why it is easier to argue, on historical grounds, that the Incarnation actually occurred than to show, on philosophical grounds, the probability of its occurrence. The historical difficulty of giving for the life, sayings, and influence of Jesus any explanation that is not harder than the Christian explanation, is very great. The discrepancy between the depth and sanity and (let me add) *shrewdness* of His moral teaching and the rampant megalomania which must lie behind His theological teaching unless He is indeed God, has never been satisfactorily got over.

Since the Incarnation, if it is a fact, holds this central position, and since we are assuming that we do not yet know it to have happened on historical grounds, we are in a position which may be illustrated by the following analogy. Let us suppose we possess parts of a novel or a symphony. Someone now brings us a newly discovered piece of manuscript and says, "This is the missing part of the work. This is the chapter on which the whole plot of the novel really turned. This is the main theme of the symphony." Our business would be to see whether the new passage, if admitted to the central place which the discoverer claimed for it, did actually illuminate all the parts we had already seen and "pull them together." Nor should we be likely to go very far wrong. The new passage, if spurious, however attractive it looked at the first glance, would become harder and harder to reconcile with the rest of the work the longer we considered the matter. But if it were genuine, then at every fresh hearing of the music or every fresh reading of the book, we should find it settling down, making itself more at home, and eliciting significance from all sorts of details in the whole work which we had hitherto neglected. Even though the new central chapter or main theme contained great difficulties in itself, we should still think it genuine provided that it continually removed difficulties elsewhere. Something like this we must do with the doctrine of the Incarnation. Here, instead of a symphony or a novel, we have the whole mass of our knowledge. The credibility will depend on the extent to which the doctrine, if accepted, can illuminate and integrate that whole mass. It is much less important that the doctrine itself should be fully comprehensible. We believe that the sun is in the

sky at midday in summer not because we can clearly
see the sun (in fact, we cannot) but because we can
see everything else.

What is not fully comprehensible lies at the center
of the doctrine: God became man. How can we
conceive eternal, self-existent spirit so combined with
a human organism as to make one person? We cannot.
But there is an analogous difficulty which we have to
put up with elsewhere. I pointed out in Chapter I how
hard it is to fit the fact of our own rational thought
into the view that we are nothing but items in the
interlocked system of Nature. Therefore I don't think
we are. I think we must admit that in every man a
created, but strictly supernatural, element has been
united with the natural animal. We cannot conceive
how. We would not imagine the product if we did not
daily experience it. Even if we left our rational thought
out of the question and considered our mere sentience
we should still meet a difficulty. How are the move-
ments of optic nerves and the disturbances they set up
in the brain related to what we mean when we say,
"I see that tree"? But it is much worse when we bring
in successful thought and the knowledge it produces.
The discrepancy between a movement of atoms in an
astronomer's cortex and his understanding that there
must be a still unobserved planet beyond Uranus, is
already so immense that the Incarnation of God
Himself, is, in one sense, scarcely more startling. We
cannot conceive how the Divine Spirit dwelled within

the created and human spirit of Jesus: but neither can we conceive how His human spirit, or that of any man, dwells within his natural organism. What we can understand, if the Christian doctrine is true, is that our own composite existence is not the sheer anomaly it might seem to be, but a faint image of the Divine Incarnation itself—the same theme in a very minor key. We can understand that if God so descends into a human spirit, and human spirit so descends into Nature, and our thoughts into our senses and passions, and if adult minds (but only the best of them) can descend into sympathy with children, and men into sympathy with beasts, then everything hangs together and the total reality, both Natural and Supernatural, in which we are living is more multifariously and subtly harmonious than we had suspected. We catch sight of a new key principle—the power of the Higher, just in so far as it is truly Higher, to come down, the power of the Greater to include the less.

God descends to reascend; descends into a womb, into death, to rise again bringing the whole ruined universe up with Him. So the seed falls into the ground and the new organism springs up. So two complete organisms commit something from themselves to the (at first) incomplete and lower life of the embryo and thence the new animal comes. So Man must submit his first desires to the death of discipline and denial if a fully formed character is to result. Die to live is the rule. The Incarnation is not

an alien marvel. It plays out clear on a celestial instrument the theme that is hinted everywhere.

Vicariousness is another key-pattern in the world.
Things are indebted to one another, dependent on one
another, sacrificed to one another. Living on one's
own resources is a thing Nature does not allow.
Horrible and lovely elements in her alike repeat this
theme: parasite and host, carnivore or prey, the tyrant
and the exploited, the mother and the child, the giver
and the receiver of alms or aid. Again, the Incarnation
is no alien miracle. The sinless dies to save the sinful.
We hear the celestial statement of the natural theme.

Of all the "dying gods" only one might be historical.
He holds bread in His hand and says, "This is my
body." But to hear Him say it men were chosen from
a race which had specially been picked out and trained
for centuries to reject the nature religions. This picking
out itself is a principle through all Nature. She is
ruthlessly selective; of many seeds one is fertile, of
many species one rational, of many individuals one a
genius.

This "choosing" of the Hebrews is undemocratic;
it is privilege, yes, but also a heavy burden. As Isaiah
recognized, the Jews suffer to heal others. The privileged are the sacrificed. And as this ambivalent
privilege is no anomaly, so the truth now taught to
the yet more privileged, more sacrificed, disciples is
no alien religion. It fulfills all paganism; but in a

milieu whence paganism is banished. The Corn-King was a mirage of Him. The Reality appears where the mirage is not. When half-gods go God arrives.

Thus the Christian doctrine floods our world with light. It simultaneously explains, refutes, and consummates paganism. It reveals the key-patterns of Nature (death, vicariousness, selection) as imperfect expressions, sometimes as depraved and morbid expressions, of things whose true and perfect form exists in supernature.

Throughout this doctrine it is, of course, implied that Nature is infected with evil. Those great key-principles which exist as modes of goodness in the Divine Life, take on, in her operations, not merely a less perfect form (that we should, on any view, expect) but forms which I have been driven to describe as morbid or depraved. And this depravity could not be totally removed without the drastic remaking of Nature. Complete human virtue could indeed banish from human life all the evils that now arise in it from vicariousness and selectiveness and retain only the good: but the wastefulness and painfulness of non-human Nature would remain—and would, of course, continue to infect human life in the form of disease. And the destiny which Christianity promises to Man clearly involves a "redemption" or "remaking" of Nature which could not stop at Man, or even at this planet. We are told that "the whole creation" is in travail, and that Man's rebirth will be the signal for hers. This gives rise to several problems, the discussion of which puts the whole doctrine of the Incarnation in a clearer light.

In the first place, we ask how the Nature created by a good God comes to be in this condition? By which question we may mean either how she comes to be imperfect—to leave "room for improvement" as the schoolmasters say in their reports—or else, how she comes to be positively depraved. If we ask the question in the first sense, the Christian answer (I think) is that God, from the first, created her such as to reach her perfection by a process in time. He made an Earth at first "without form and void" and brought it by degrees to its perfection. In that sense a certain degree of "evolutionism" or "developmentalism" is inherent in Christianity. So much for Nature's imperfection; her positive depravity calls for a very different explanation. According to the Christians this is all due to sin: the sin both of men and of powerful, nonhuman beings, supernatural but created.

The sin, both of men and of angels, was rendered possible by the fact that God gave them free will: thus surrendering a portion of His omnipotence (it is again a deathlike or descending movement) because He saw that from a world of free creatures, even though they fell, He could work out (and this is the reascent) a deeper happiness and a fuller splendor than any world of automata would admit.

Another question that arises is this. If the redemption of Man is the beginning of Nature's redemption as a whole, must we then conclude after all that Man is the most important thing in Nature? If I had to answer "Yes" to this question I should not be embarrassed. Supposing Man to be the only rational animal in the universe, then (as has been shown) his small size and the small size of the globe he inhabits would not make it ridiculous to regard him as the hero of the cosmic drama: Jack after all is the smallest character in "Jack and the Beanstalk." But suppose Man is only one among a myriad of rational species, and is the only one that has fallen. Because he has fallen, for him God does the great deed; just as in the parable it is the one lost sheep for whom the shepherd hunts. Let Man's pre-eminence or solitude be one not of superiority but of misery and evil: then, all the more, Man will be the very species into which Mercy will descend. For this prodigal the fatted calf, or, to speak more suitably, the eternal Lamb, is killed. But once the Son of God, drawn hither not by our merits but by our unworthiness, has put on human nature, then our species (whatever it may have been before) does become in one sense the central fact in all Nature: our species, rising after its long descent, will drag all Nature up with it because in our species the Lord of Nature is now included. And it would be all of a piece with what we already know if ninety-and-nine righteous races inhabiting distant planets that circle distant suns, and needing no redemption on their own account, were remade and glorified by the glory which had descended into our race.

This doctrine of a universal redemption spreading outward from the redemption of Man, mythological as it will seem to modern minds, is in reality far more philosophical than any theory which holds that God, having once entered Nature, should leave her, and leave her substantially unchanged, or that the glorification of one creature could be realized without the glorification of the whole system. God never undoes anything but evil, never does good to undo it again. The union between God and Nature in the Person of Christ admits no divorce. He will not *go out of* Nature again, and she must be glorified in all ways which this miraculous union demands. When spring comes it "leaves no corner of the land untouched"; even a pebble dropped in a pond sends circles to the margin.

The question we want to ask about Man's "central" position in this drama is really on a level with the disciples' question, "Which of them was the greatest?" It is the sort of question which God does not answer. If from Man's point of view the re-creation of non-human and even inanimate Nature appears a mere by-product of his own redemption, then equally from some remote, nonhuman point of view man's redemption may seem merely the preliminary to this more widely diffused springtime, and the very permission of Man's fall may be supposed to have had that larger end in view. Both attitudes will be right if they will consent to drop the words *mere* and *merely*. Where a God who is totally purposive and totally foreseeing acts upon a Nature which is totally interlocked, there can be no accidents or loose ends, nothing whatever of which we can safely use the word *merely*. Nothing is "merely a by-product" of anything else. All results are intended from the first. What is subservient from one point of view is the main purpose from another. No thing or event is first or highest in a sense which forbids it to be also last and lowest. The partner who bows to Man in one movement of the dance receives Man's reverences in another. To be high or central means to abdicate continually: to be low means to be raised: all good masters are servants: God washes the feet of men. The concepts we usually bring to the consideration of such matters are miserably political and prosaic.

For this reason I do not think it at all likely that there have been many Incarnations to redeem many different kinds of creature. One's sense of *style*—of the divine idiom—rejects it. The suggestion of mass-production and of waiting queues comes from a level of thought which is here hopelessly inadequate. If natural creatures other than Man have sinned we must believe that they are redeemed: but God's Incarnation as Man will be one unique act in the drama of total redemption.

It ought to be noticed at this stage that the Christian doctrine, if accepted, involves a particular view of Death. Human death, according to the Christians, is a result of human sin; Man, as originally created, was immune from it: Man, when redeemed, and recalled to a new life (which will in some undefined sense, be a bodily life) in the midst of a more organic and more fully obedient Nature, will be immune from it again. This doctrine is of course simply nonsense if a man is nothing but a natural organism. But if he were, then, as we have seen, all thoughts would be equally nonsensical, for all would have nonrational causes. Man must therefore be a composite being—a natural organism tenanted by, or in a state of *symbiosis* with, a supernatural spirit. The Christian doctrine, startling as it must seem to those who have not fully cleared their minds of Naturalism, states that the relations which we now observe between that spirit and that organism, are abnormal or pathological ones. At present, spirit can retain its foothold against the incessant counterattacks of Nature (both physiological and psychological) only by perpetual vigilance, and physiological Nature always defeats it in the end. Sooner or later it becomes unable to resist the disintegrating process at work in the body, and death ensues.

A little later the natural organism (for it does not long enjoy its triumph) is similarly conquered by merely physical Nature and returns to the inorganic.

But, in the Christian view, this was not always so. The spirit was once not a garrison, maintaining its post with difficulty in a hostile Nature, but was fully "at home" with its organism, like a king in his own country or a rider on his own horse—or better still, as the human part of a centaur was "at home" with the equine part. Where spirit's power over the organism was complete and unresisted, death would never occur. No doubt, spirit's permanent triumph over natural forces which, if left to themselves, would kill the organism, would involve a continued miracle: but only the same sort of miracle which occurs every day—for whenever we think rationally we are, by direct spiritual power, forcing certain atoms in our brain and certain psychological tendencies in our natural soul to do what they would never have done if left to Nature.

So much for the sense in which human death is the result of sin and the triumph of Satan. But it is also the means of redemption from sin, God's medicine for Man and His weapon against Satan. In a general way it is not difficult to understand how the same thing can be a master stroke on the part of one combatant and also the very means whereby the superior combatant defeats him. Every good general, every good chess player, takes what is precisely the strong point of his opponent's plan and makes it the pivot of his own plan. Take that castle of mine if you insist. It was not my original intention that you should—indeed,

I thought you would have had more sense. But take it by all means. For now I move thus ... and thus ... and it is mate in three moves. Something like this must be supposed to have happened about Death. Do not say that such metaphors are too trivial to illustrate so high a matter: the unnoticed mechanical and mineral metaphors which, in this age, will dominate our whole minds (without being recognized as metaphors at all) the moment we relax our vigilance against them, must be incomparably less adequate.

And one can see how it might have happened. The Enemy persuades Man to rebel against God: Man, by doing so, loses power to control that other rebellion which the Enemy now raises in Man's organism (both psychical and physical) against Man's spirit: just as that organism, in its turn, loses power to maintain itself against the rebellion of the inorganic. In that way, Satan produced human death. But when God created Man he gave him such a constitution that if the highest part of it rebelled against Himself, it would be bound to lose control over the lower parts: that is, in the long run to suffer death. This provision may be regarded equally as a punitive sentence ("In the day ye eat of that fruit ye shall die"), as a mercy, and as a safety device. It is punishment because death—that death of which Martha says to Christ, "But ... Sir ... it'll *smell*"—is horror and ignominy. ("I am not so much afraid of death as ashamed of it," said Sir Thomas Browne.) It is mercy because by willing and humble surrender to it Man undoes his act of rebellion and makes even this depraved and monstrous mode of death an instance of that higher and mystical Death which is eternally good and a necessary ingredient in the highest life. Our enemy, so welcomed, becomes our servant: bodily death, the monster, becomes blessed spiritual Death to self, if the spirit so wills—or rather if it allows the Spirit of the willingly dying God so to will in it. It is a safety device because, once Man has fallen, natural immortality would be the one utterly hopeless destiny for him. Aided to the surrender that he must make by no external necessity of death, free (if you call it freedom) to rivet faster and faster about himself through unending centuries the chains of his own pride and lust and of the nightmare civilizations which these would build up in ever-increasing power and complication, he would progress from being merely a fallen man to being a fiend, possibly beyond all modes of redemption. This danger was averted. The sentence that those who ate of the forbidden fruit would be driven away from the Tree of Life was implicit in the composite nature with which Man was created. But to convert this penal death into the means of eternal life—to add to its negative and preventive function a positive and saving function—it was further necessary that death should be *accepted*. Humanity must embrace death freely, submit to it with total humility, drink it to the dregs, and so convert it into that mystical Death which is the secret of Life. But only a Man who did not need to have been a Man at all unless He had chosen, only one who served in our sad regiment as a volunteer, yet also only one who was perfectly a Man, could perform this perfect dying; and thus (which way you put it is unimportant) either defeat Death or redeem it. He tasted Death on behalf of all others. He is the representative "Die-er" of the universe: and for that very reason the Resurrection and the Life. Or conversely, because He truly lives, He truly dies, for that is the very pattern of reality. Because the higher can descend into the lower, He who from all eternity has been incessantly plunging Himself in the blessed death of self-surrender to the Father can also most fully descend into the horrible and (for us) involuntary death of the body. The whole Miracle, far from denying what we already know of reality, writes the comment which makes that crabbed text plain: or rather, proves itself to be the text on which Nature was only the commentary. In science we have been reading only the notes to a poem; in Christianity we find the poem itself.

With this our sketch of the Grand Miracle may end. Its credibility does not lie in obviousness. Pessimism, Optimism, Pantheism, Materialism, all have this "obvious" attraction. Each is confirmed at the first glance by multitudes of facts: later on, each meets insuperable obstacles. The doctrine of the Incarnation works into our minds quite differently. It digs beneath the surface, works through the rest of our knowledge by unexpected channels, harmonizes best with our deepest apprehensions and our "second thoughts," and in union with these undermines our superficial opinions. It has little to say to the man who is still certain that everything is going to the dogs, or that everything is getting better and better, or that everything is God, or that everything is electricity. Its hour comes when these wholesale creeds have begun to fail us. Whether the thing really happened is a historical question. But when you turn to history, you will not demand for it that kind and degree of evidence which you would rightly demand for something intrinsically improbable; only that kind and degree which you demand for something which, if accepted, illuminates and orders all other phenomena, explains both our laughter and our logic, our fear of the dead and our knowledge that it is somehow good to die, and which at one stroke covers what multitudes of separate theories will hardly cover for us if this is rejected.

VIII. *Miracles of the Old Creation*

The Son can do nothing of himself, but what he seeth the Father do.

John 5:19

If we open such books as Grimm's *Fairy Tales* or Ovid's *Metamorphoses* or the Italian epics we find ourselves in a world of miracles so diverse that they can hardly be classified. Beasts turn into men and men into beasts or trees, trees talk, ships become goddesses, and a magic ring can cause tables richly spread with food to appear in solitary places. If such things really happened they would, I suppose, show that Nature was being invaded. But they would show that she was being invaded by an alien power. The fitness of the Christian miracles lies in the fact that they show invasion by a Power which is not alien. They are what might be expected to happen when she is invaded not simply by a god, but by the God of Nature. They proclaim that He who has come is not merely a king, but *the* King, her King and ours.

It is this which, to my mind, puts the Christian miracles in a different class from most other miracles. I do not think that it is the duty of a Christian apologist (as many skeptics suppose) to disprove all stories of the miraculous which fall outside the Christian records, nor of a Christian man to disbelieve them. I am in no way committed to the assertion that God has never worked miracles through and for pagans or never permitted created supernatural beings to do so. If, as Tacitus, Suetonius, and Dion Cassius relate, Vespasian performed two cures, and if modern doctors tell me that they could not have been performed without miracle, I have no objection. If it can be shown that one particular Roman emperor—and, let us admit, a fairly good emperor as emperors go— once was empowered to do a miracle, we must of course put up with the fact. But it would remain a quite isolated and anomalous fact. Nothing comes of it, nothing leads up to it, it establishes no body of doctrine, explains nothing, is connected with nothing. Sometimes the credibility of the miracles is in an inverse ratio to the credibility of the religion. Thus miracles are (in late documents, I believe) recorded of the Buddha. But what could be more absurd than that he who came to teach us that Nature is an illusion from which we must escape should occupy himself in producing effects on the natural level—that he who comes to wake us from a nightmare should *add* to the nightmare? The more we respect his teaching the less we could accept his miracles.

The miracles of Christ can be classified in two ways. The first system yields the classes (1) Miracles of Fertility (2) Miracles of Healing (3) Miracles of Destruction (4) Miracles of Dominion over the Inorganic (5) Miracles of Reversal (6) Miracles of Perfecting or Glorification. The second system, which cuts across the first, yields two classes only: they are (1) Miracles of the Old Creation, and (2) Miracles of the New Creation.

I contend that in all these miracles alike the incarnate God does suddenly and locally something that God has done or will do in general. Each miracle writes for us in small letters something that God has already written, or will write, in letters almost too large to be noticed, across the whole canvas of Nature. They focus at a particular point either God's actual, or His future, operations on the universe. When they reproduce operations we have already seen on the large scale they are Miracles of the Old Creation: when they focus those which are still to come they are miracles of the New. Not one of them is isolated or anomalous: each carries the signature of the God whom we know through conscience and from Nature.

Another way of expressing the real character of the Miracles would be to say that though isolated from other actions, they are not isolated in either of the two ways we are apt to suppose. They are not, on the one hand, isolated from other Divine Acts: they do, close and small and, as it were, in focus, what God at other times does so large that men do not attend to it. Neither are they isolated exactly as we suppose from other human acts: they anticipate powers which all men will have when they also are "sons" of God and enter into that "glorious liberty." For the powers promised to redeemed man seem almost unlimited.[1] Christ, reascending from His great dive, is bringing up human nature with Him. Where He goes, it goes too. It will be made "like him." [2] Christ's isolation is not that of a prodigy but of a pioneer. He is the first of His kind; He will not be the last.

Let us return to our classification and, first, to Miracles of *Fertility*. The earliest of these was the conversion of water into wine at the wedding feast in Cana. This miracle proclaims that the God of all wine is present. The vine is one of the blessings sent by Jahweh: He is the reality behind the false god Bacchus. Every year, as part of the natural order, God makes wine. He does so by creating a vegetable organism that can turn water, soil, and sunlight into a juice which will, under proper conditions, become wine. Thus, in a certain sense, He constantly turns water into wine, for wine, like all drinks, is but water modified. Once, and in one year only, God, now incarnate, short-circuits the process: makes wine in a moment; uses earthenware jars instead of vegetable fibers to hold the water. But He uses them to do what He is always doing. The Miracle consists in the short cut; but the event to which it leads is the usual one. If the thing happened, then we know that what has come into Nature is no antinatural spirit, no God who loves tragedy and tears and fasting for *their own sake* (however He may permit or demand them for special purposes) but the God of Israel who has through all these centuries given us wine to gladden the heart of man.

Other miracles that fall in this class are the two instances of miraculous feeding. They involve the multiplication of a little bread and a little fish into much bread and much fish. Once in the desert Satan had tempted Jesus to make bread of stones: He refused the suggestion. "The Son does nothing except what He sees the Father do"; perhaps one may without boldness surmise that the direct change from stone to bread appeared to the Son to be not quite in the hereditary style. Little bread into much bread is quite a different matter. Every year God makes a little corn into much corn: the seed is sown and there is an increase. And men say, according to their several fashions, "It is the laws of Nature," or, "It is Ceres, it is Adonis, it is the Corn-King." But the laws of Nature are only a pattern: nothing will come of them unless they can, so to speak, take over the universe as a going concern. And as for Adonis, no man can tell us where he died or when he rose again. Here, at the feeding of the five thousand, is He whom we have ignorantly worshiped: the *real* Corn-King who will die once and rise once at Jerusalem during the term of office of Pontius Pilate.

That same day He also multiplied fish. Look down into every bay and almost every river. This swarming,

Theory of Timing element ?

undulating fecundity shows He is still at work "thronging the seas with spawn innumerable." The ancients had a god called Genius; the god of animal and human fertility, the patron of gynecology, embryology, and the marriage bed—the "genial" bed as they called it after its god Genius. But Genius is only another mask for the God of Israel, for it was He who at the beginning commanded all species "to be fruitful and multiply and replenish the earth." And now, that day, at the feeding of the thousands, incarnate God does the same: does close and small, under His human hands, a workman's hands, what He has always been doing in the seas, the lakes, and the little brooks.

With this we stand on the threshold of that Miracle which for some reason proves hardest of all for the modern mind to accept. I can understand the man who denies miracles altogether: but what is one to make of people who will believe other miracles and "draw the line" at the Virgin Birth? Is it that for all their lip service to the laws of Nature there is only one natural process in which they really believe? Or is it that they think they see in this miracle a slur upon sexual intercourse (though they might just as well see in the feeding of the five thousand an insult to bakers) and that sexual intercourse is the one thing still venerated in this unvenerating age? In reality the Miracle is no less, and no more, surprising than any other.

Perhaps the best way to approach it is from the re-

mark I saw in one of the most archaic of our anti-god
papers. The remark was that Christians believed in a
God who had "committed adultery with the wife of a
Jewish carpenter." The writer was probably merely
"letting off steam" and did not really think that God,
in the Christian story, had assumed human form and
lain with a mortal woman, as Zeus lay with Alcmena.
But if one had to answer this person, one would have
to say that if you called the miraculous conception
divine adultery you would be driven to find a similar
divine adultery in the conception of every child—nay,
of every animal too. I am sorry to use expressions
which will offend pious ears, but I do not know how
else to make my point.

In a normal act of generation the father has no
creative function. A microscopic particle of matter
from his body, and a microscopic particle from the
woman's body, meet. And with that there passes the
color of his hair and the hanging lower lip of her
grandfather and the form of humanity in all its complexity of bones, sinews, nerves, liver and heart, and
the form of those prehuman organisms which the
embryo will recapitulate in the womb. Behind every
spermatozoon lies the whole history of the universe:
locked within it lies no inconsiderable part of the
world's future. The weight or drive behind it is the
momentum of the whole interlocked event which we
call Nature up to date. And we know now that the
"laws of Nature" cannot supply that momentum. If

we believe that God created Nature, that momentum comes from Him. The human father is merely an instrument, a carrier, often an unwilling carrier, always simply the last in a long line of carriers—a line that stretches back far beyond his ancestors into prehuman and preorganic deserts of time, back to the creation of matter itself. That line is in God's hand. It is the instrument by which He normally creates a man. For He is the reality behind both Genius and Venus; no woman ever conceived a child, no mare a foal, without Him. But once, and for a special purpose, He dispensed with that long line which is His instrument: once His life-giving finger touched a woman without passing through the ages of interlocked events. Once the great glove of Nature was taken off His hand. His naked hand touched her. There was of course a unique reason for it. That time He was creating not simply a man but the Man who was to be Himself: was creating Man anew: was beginning, at this divine and human point, the New Creation of all things.

The Miracles of *Healing,* to which I turn next, are now in a peculiar position. Men are ready to admit that many of them happened but are inclined to deny that they were miraculous. The symptoms of very many diseases can be aped by hysteria, and hysteria can often be cured by "suggestion." My own view is that it would be unreasonable to ask a person who has not yet embraced Christianity in its entirety to allow that all the healings mentioned in the Gospels were miracles—that is, that they go beyond the possibilities of human "suggestion." It is for the doctors to decide as regards each particular case—supposing that the narratives are sufficiently detailed to allow even probable diagnosis. We have here a good example to what was said in an earlier chapter. So far from belief in miracles depending upon ignorance of natural law, we are here finding for ourselves that ignorance of law makes miracle unascertainable.

Without deciding in detail which of the healings must (apart from acceptance of the Christian faith) be regarded as miraculous, we can however indicate the kind of miracle involved. Its character can easily be obscured by the somewhat magical view which many people still take of ordinary and medical healing. There is a sense in which no doctor ever heals. The doctors themselves would be the first to admit this. The magic is not in the medicine but in the patient's body—in the *vis medicatrix naturae,* the recuperative or self-corrective energy of Nature. What the treatment does is to stimulate natural functions or to remove what hinders them. We speak, for convenience, of the doctor or the dressing healing a cut. But in another sense every cut heals itself: no cut can be healed in a corpse. That same mysterious force which we call gravitational when it steers the planets, and biochemical when it heals a live body, is the efficient cause of all recoveries. And that energy proceeds from God in the first instance. All who are cured are cured by Him in the sense that their very tissues are repaired by the far-descended energy which, flowing from Him, energizes the whole system of Nature. But once He did it visibly to the sick in Palestine, a Man meeting with men. What in its general operations we refer to laws of Nature or once referred to Apollo or Asclepius thus reveals itself.

Christ's single Miracle of Destruction, the withering of the fig tree, has proved troublesome to some people, but I think its significance is plain enough. The miracle is an acted parable, a symbol of God's sentence on all that is "fruitless" and specially, no doubt, on the official Judaism of that age. That is its moral significance. As a miracle, it again does in focus, repeats small and close, what God does constantly and throughout Nature. We have seen in the previous chapter how God, twisting Satan's weapon out of his hand, had become, since the Fall, the God even of human death. But much more, and perhaps ever since the creation, He has been the God of the death of organisms. In both cases, though in somewhat different ways, He is the God of Death because He is the God of Life: the God of human death because through it increase of life now comes—the God of merely organic death because death is part of the very mode by which organic life spreads itself out in Time and yet remains new. A forest a thousand years deep is still collectively alive because some trees are dying and others are growing up. His human face, turned with negation in its eyes upon that one fig tree, did once what his unincarnate action does to all trees. No tree died that year in Palestine, or any year anywhere, except because God did—or rather ceased to do—something to it.

All the miracles which we have considered so far are Miracles of the Old Creation. In all of them we see the Divine Man focusing for us what the God of Nature has already done on a larger scale. In our next class, the Miracles of Dominion over the Inorganic, we find some that are of the Old Creation and some that are of the New. When Christ stills the storm he does what God has often done before. God made Nature such that there would be both storms and calms: in that way all storms (except those that are still going on at this moment) have been stilled by God. It is unphilosophical, if you have once accepted the Grand Miracle, to reject the stilling of the storm. There is really no difficulty about adapting the weather conditions of the rest of the world to this one miraculous calm. I myself can still a storm in a room by shutting the window. Nature must make the best she can of it. And to do her justice she makes no trouble at all. The whole system, far from being thrown out of gear (which is what some nervous people seem to think a miracle would do) digests the new situation as easily as an elephant digests a drop of water. She is, as I have said before, an accomplished hostess. But when Christ walks on the water we have a Miracle of the New Creation. God had not made the Old Nature, the world before the Incarnation, of such a kind that water would support a human body. This miracle is the foretaste of a Nature that is still in the future. The New Creation is just breaking in. For a moment it looks as if it were going to spread. For a moment two men are living in that new world. St. Peter also walks on the water—a pace or two: then his trust fails him and he sinks. He is back in Old Nature. That momentary glimpse was a snowdrop of a miracle. The snowdrops show that we have turned the corner of the year. Summer is coming. But it is a long way off and the snowdrops do not last long.

The Miracles of Reversal all belong to the New Creation. It is a Miracle of Reversal when the dead are raised. Old Nature knows nothing of this process: it involves playing backward a film that we have always seen played forward. The one or two instances of it in the Gospels are early flowers—what we call spring flowers, because they are prophetic, although they really bloom while it is still winter. And the Miracles of Perfecting or of Glory—the Transfiguration, the Resurrection, and the Ascension—are even more emphatically of the New Creation. These are the true spring, or even the summer, of the world's new year. The Captain, the forerunner, is already in May or June, though His followers on earth are still living in the frosts and east winds of Old Nature—for "spring comes slowly up this way."

IX. *Miracles of the New Creation*

> Beware; for fiends in triumph laugh
> O'er him who learns the truth by half!
> Beware; for God will not endure
> For men to make their hope more pure
> Than His good promise, or require
> Another than the five-stringed lyre[1]
> Which He has vowed again to the hands
> Devout of him who understands
> To tune it justly here!
>
> c. PATMORE, *The Victories of Love*

In the earliest days of Christianity an "apostle" was first and foremost a man who claimed to be an eyewitness of the Resurrection. Only a few days after the Crucifixion when two candidates were nominated for the vacancy created by the treachery of Judas, their qualification was that they had known Jesus personally both before and after His death and could offer firsthand evidence of the Resurrection in addressing the outer world (Acts 1:22). A few days later St. Peter, preaching the first Christian sermon, makes the same claim—"God raised Jesus, of which we all (we Christians) are witnesses" (Acts 2:32). In the first Letter to the Corinthians St. Paul bases his claim to apostleship on the same ground—"Am I not an apostle? Have I not seen the Lord Jesus?"

As this qualification suggests, to preach Christianity meant primarily to preach the Resurrection. Thus people who had heard only fragments of St. Paul's teaching at Athens got the impression that he was talking about two new gods, Jesus and Anastasis (that is, Resurrection) (Acts 17:18). The Resurrection is the central theme in every Christian sermon reported in the Acts. The Resurrection, and its consequences, were the "gospel" or good news which the Christians brought: what we call the "Gospels," the narratives of our Lord's life and death, were composed later for the benefit of those who had already accepted the *gospel*. They were in no sense the basis of Christianity: they were written for those already converted. The Miracle of the Resurrection, and the theology of that miracle, comes first: the biography comes later as a comment on it. Nothing could be more unhistorical than to pick out selected sayings of Christ from the Gospels and to regard those as the datum and the rest of the New Testament as a construction upon it. The first fact in the history of Christendom is a number of people who say they have seen the Resurrection. If they had died without making anyone else believe this "gospel" no Gospels would ever have been written.

It is very important to be clear about what these people meant. When modern writers talk of the Resurrection they usually mean one particular moment—the discovery of the Empty Tomb and the appearance of Jesus a few yards away from it. The story of that moment is what Christian apologists now chiefly try to support and skeptics chiefly try to impugn. But this almost exclusive concentration on the first five minutes or so of the Resurrection would have astonished the earliest Christian teachers. In claiming to have seen the Resurrection they were not necessarily claiming to have seen *that*. What they were claiming was that they had all, at one time or another, met Jesus during the six or seven weeks that followed His death.

The "Resurrection" to which they bore witness was, in fact, not the action of rising from the dead but the state of having risen; a state, as they held, attested by intermittent meetings during a limited period (except for the special, and in some ways different, meeting vouchsafed to St. Paul). This termination of the period is important, for, as we shall see, there is no possibility of isolating the doctrine of the Resurrection from that of the Ascension.

The next point to notice is that the Resurrection was not regarded simply or chiefly as evidence for the immortality of the soul. Such a view cannot at any point be reconciled with the language of the New Testament. On such a view Christ would simply have done what all men do when they die: the only novelty would have been that in His case we were allowed to see it happening. But there is not in Scripture the faintest suggestion that the Resurrection was new evidence for something that had *in fact* been always happening. The New Testament writers speak as if Christ's achievement in rising from the dead was the first event of its kind in the whole history of the universe. He is the "first fruits," the "pioneer of life." He has forced open a door that had been locked since the death of the first man.

I do not mean, of course, that the writers of the New Testament disbelieved in "survival." On the contrary they believed in it so readily that Jesus on more than one occasion had to assure them that He was not a ghost. From the earliest times the Jews, like many other nations, had believed that man possessed a "soul" or *Nephesh* separable from the body, which went at death into the shadowy world called *Sheol*: a land of forgetfulness and imbecility where none called upon Jehovah any more, a land half unreal and melancholy like the Hades of the Greeks or the *Niflheim* of the Norsemen. From it shades could return and appear to the living, as Samuel's shade had done at the command of the Witch of Endor. In much more recent times there had arisen a more cheerful belief that the righteous passed at death to "Heaven." Both doctrines are doctrines of "the immortality of the soul" as a Greek or a modern Englishmen understands it: and both are quite irrelevant to the story of the Resurrection. The writers look upon this event as an absolute novelty. Quite clearly they do not think they have been haunted by a ghost from Sheol, nor even that they have had a vision of a "soul" in "Heaven." It must be clearly understood that if the Psychical Researchers succeeded in proving "survival" and showed that the Resurrection was an instance of it, they would not be supporting the Christian faith but refuting it. If that were all that had happened the original "gospel" would have been untrue. What the apostles claimed to have seen did not corroborate, nor exclude, and had indeed nothing to do with, either the doctrine of "Heaven" or the doctrine of Sheol. In so far as it corroborated anything it corroborated a third Jewish belief which is quite distinct from both these. This third doctrine taught that in "the day of Jahweh" peace would be restored and world dominion given to Israel under a righteous King: and that when this happened the righteous dead, or some of them, would come back to earth—not as floating wraiths but as solid men who cast shadows in the sunlight and made a noise when they tramped the floors. What the apostles thought they had seen was, if not that, at any rate a lonely first instance of that: the first movement of a great wheel beginning to turn in the direction opposite to that which all men hitherto had observed. Of all the ideas entertained by man about death it is this one, and this one only, which the story of the Resurrection tends to confirm. If the story is false, then it is this Hebrew myth of resurrection which begot it. If the story is true, then the hint and anticipation of the truth is to be found not in popular ideas about ghosts nor in eastern doctrines of reincarnation nor in philosophical speculations about the immortality of the soul, but exclusively in the Hebrew prophecies of the return, the restoration, the great reversal. Immortality simply as immortality is irrelevant to the Christian claim.

The risen Christ vigorously asserts that He is corporeal (Luke 24:39-40) and eats broiled fish. It is at this point that the modern reader becomes uncomfortable. He becomes more uncomfortable still at the words, "Don't touch me; I have not yet gone up to the Father" (John 20:17). For voices and apparitions we are, in some measure, prepared. But what is this that must not be touched? What is all this about going "up" to the Father? These discomforts arise because the story the apostles actually had to tell begins at this point to conflict with the story we expect and are determined beforehand to read into their narrative.

We expect them to tell of a risen life which is purely "spiritual" in the negative sense of that word: that is, we use the word "spiritual" to mean not what it is but what it is not. We mean a life without space, without history, without environment, with no sensuous elements in it. That being so, all references to the risen *body* make us uneasy; they raise awkward questions, for as long as we hold the negatively spiritual view, we have not really been believing in that body at all. We have thought (whether we acknowledged it or not) that the body was not objective: that it was an appearance sent by God to assure the disciples of truths otherwise incommunicable. But what truths? If the truth is that after death there comes a negatively spiritual life, an eternity of mystical experience, what more misleading way of communicating it could possibly be found than the appearance of a human form which eats broiled fish? Again, on such a view, the body would really be a hallucination. And any theory of hallucination breaks down on the fact (and if it is invention it is the oddest invention that ever entered the mind of man) that on three separate occasions this hallucination was not immediately recognized as Jesus (Luke 24:13-31; John 20:15, 21:4). Even granting that God sent a holy hallucination to teach truths already widely believed without it, far more easily taught by other methods, and certain to be completely obscured by this, might we not at least hope that He would get the face of the hallucination *right*? Is He who made all faces such a bungler that He cannot even work up a recognizable likeness of the Man who was Himself?

It is at this point that awe and trembling fall upon us as we read the records. If the story is false, it is at least a much stranger story than we expected. If the story is true, then a wholly new mode of being has arisen in the universe.

The body, which lives in that new mode is like, and yet unlike, the body Jesus' friends knew before the execution. It is differently related to space and probably to time, but by no means cut off from all relation to them. It can perform the animal act of eating. It is so related to matter, as we know it, that it can be touched, though at first it had better not be touched. It has also a history before it which is in view from the first moment of the Resurrection; it is presently going to become different or go somewhere else. That is why the story of the Ascension cannot be separated from that of the Resurrection. All the accounts suggest that the appearances of the Risen Body came to an end; some describe an abrupt end about six weeks after the death. And they describe this abrupt end in a way which presents greater difficulties to the modern mind than any other part of Scripture. For here, surely we get the implication of all those primitive crudities to which I have said that Christians are not committed: the vertical ascent like a balloon, the local Heaven, the decorated chair to the right of the Father's throne. "He was caught up into the sky (*ouranos*)," says St. Mark's Gospel, "and sat down at the right hand of God." "He was lifted up," says the author of Acts, "and a cloud cut him off from their sight."

It is true that if we wish to get rid of these embarrassing passages we have the means to do so. The Marcan one probably formed no part of the earliest text of St. Mark's Gospel: and you may add that the Ascension, though constantly implied throughout the New Testament, is described only in these two places. Can we then simply drop the Ascension story? The answer is that we can do so only if we regard the Resurrection appearances as those of a ghost or hallucination. A phantom can just fade away; but an objective entity must go somewhere—something must happen to it. And if the Risen Body were not objective, then all of us (Christian or not) must invent some explanation for the disappearance of the corpse.

The records represent Christ as passing after death (as no man had passed before) neither into a purely, that is, negatively, "spiritual" mode of existence nor into a "natural" life such as we know, but into a life which has its own, new Nature. It represents Him as withdrawing six weeks later, into some different mode of existence. It says—He says—that He goes "to prepare a place for us." This presumably means that He is about to create that whole new Nature which will provide the environment or conditions for His glorified humanity and, in Him, for ours. The picture is not what we expected—though whether it is less or more probable and philosophical on that account is another question. It is not the picture of an escape from any and every kind of Nature into some unconditioned and utterly transcendent life. It is the picture of a new human nature, and a new Nature in general, being brought into existence. We must, indeed, believe the Risen Body to be extremely different from the mortal body: but the existence, in that new state, of anything that could in any sense be described as "body" at all, involves some sort of spatial relations and in the long run a whole new universe. That is the picture—not of unmaking but of remaking.

And yet the very way in which this new Nature

begins to shine in has a certain affinity with the habits of old Nature. In Nature as we know her, things tend to be anticipated. Nature is fond of "false dawns," of precursors: thus, as I said before, some flowers come before true spring: submen (the evolutionists would have it) before the true men. So, here also, we get Law before Gospel, animal sacrifices foreshadowing the great sacrifice of God to God, the Baptist before the Messiah, and those "Miracles of the New Creation" which come before the Resurrection. Christ's walking on the water, and His raising of Lazarus fall in this class. Both give us hints of what the New Nature will be like.

In the Walking on the Water we see the relations of spirit and Nature so altered that Nature can be made to do whatever spirit pleases. This new obedience of Nature is, of course, not to be separated even in thought from spirit's own obedience to the Father of Spirits. Apart from that proviso such obedience by Nature, if it were possible, would result in chaos: the evil dream of Magic arises from finite spirit's longing to get that power without paying that price. The evil reality of lawless applied science (which is Magic's son and heir) is actually reducing large tracts of Nature to disorder and sterility at this very moment. I do not know how radically Nature herself would need to be altered to make her thus obedient to spirits, when spirits have become wholly obedient to their source.

The raising of Lazarus differs from the Resurrection

of Christ Himself because Lazarus, so far as we know, was not raised to a new and more glorious mode of existence but merely restored to the sort of life he had had before. The fitness of the miracle lies in the fact that He who will raise all men at the general resurrection here does it small and close, and in an inferior —a merely anticipatory—fashion. For the mere restoration of Lazarus is as inferior in splendor to the *glorious* resurrection of the New Humanity as stone jars are to the green and growing vine or five little barley loaves to all the waving bronze and gold of a fat valley ripe for harvest. The resuscitation of Lazarus, so far as we can see, is simple reversal: a series of changes working in the direction opposite to that we have always experienced. At death, matter which has been organic, begins to flow away into the inorganic, to be finally scattered and used (some of it) by other organisms. The resurrection of Lazarus involves the reverse process. The general resurrection involves the reverse process universalized—a rush of matter toward organization at the call of spirits which require it. The unity of our bodies does not, even in this present life, consist in retaining the same particles.

But the miracle of Lazarus, though only anticipatory in one sense, belongs emphatically to the New Creation, for nothing is more definitely excluded by Old Nature than any return to *a status quo*. The pattern of Death and Rebirth never restores the previous individual organism. And similarly, on the inorganic level, we are told that Nature never restores order where disorder has once occurred. "Shuffling," said Professor Eddington, "is the thing Nature never undoes." Hence we live in a universe where organisms are always getting more disordered. These laws between them—irreversible death and irreversible entropy—cover almost the whole of what St. Paul calls the "vanity" of Nature: her futility, her ruinousness. And the film is never reversed.

But entropy by its very character assures us that though it may be the universal rule in the Nature we know, it cannot be universal absolutely. If a man says "Humpty Dumpty is falling," you see at once that this is not a complete story. The bit you have been told implies both a later chapter in which Humpty Dumpty will have reached the ground, and an earlier chapter in which he was still seated on the wall. A Nature which is "running down" cannot be the whole story. A clock can't run down unless it has been wound up. Humpty Dumpty can't fall off a wall which never existed. If a Nature which disintegrates order were the whole of reality, where would she find any order to disintegrate? Thus on any view there must have been a time when processes the reverse of those we now see were going on: a time of winding up. The Christian claim is that those days are not gone forever. Humpty Dumpty is going to be replaced on the wall

—at least in the sense that what has died is going to recover life, probably in the sense that the inorganic universe is going to be reordered.

The Transfiguration or "Metamorphosis" of Jesus is also, no doubt, an anticipatory glimpse of something to come. He is seen conversing with two of the ancient dead. The change which His own human form had undergone is described as one to luminosity, to "shining whiteness." A similar whiteness characterizes His appearance at the beginning of the book of Revelation. One rather curious detail is that this shining or whiteness affected His clothes as much as His body. St. Mark indeed mentions the clothes more explicitly than the face, and adds, with his inimitable naïveté, that "no laundry could do anything like it." Taken by itself this episode bears all the marks of a "vision": that is, of an experience which, though it may be divinely sent and may reveal great truth, yet is not, objectively speaking, the experience it seems to be. But if the theory of "vision" (or holy hallucination) will not cover the Resurrection appearances, it would be only a multiplying of hypotheses to introduce it here. We do not know to what phase or feature of the New Creation this episode points. It may reveal some special glorifying of Christ's manhood at some phase of its history (since history it apparently has) or it may reveal the glory which that manhood always has in its New Creation: it may even reveal a glory which all risen men will inherit. We do not know.

Indeed we can know almost nothing about the New Nature. Nearly all we are told about it must therefore be metaphorical. But not quite all. That is where the New Testament jerks us back like a tether. The local appearances, the eating, the touching, the insistence on the corporeal, show the New Nature to be, at points, bafflingly interlocked with the old. The idea of a New Nature is shocking to our habits of thought. We are prepared for a one-floored reality, like the Naturalists'; this present Nature and nothing above it. We are prepared for a two-floored reality; Nature, and above her a timeless, spaceless, bodiless spirituality, "white radiance of eternity." But not for "floors" in between. This, however, may be mere prejudice. There can be no evidence that God never made, nor will make, more Natures than one. There might be Natures piled upon Natures each relatively supernatural to the one below it.

Let us confess that probably every Christian now alive finds a difficulty in reconciling the two things he has been told about "Heaven"—that it is, on the one hand, a life in Christ, a vision of God, a ceaseless adoration, and that it is, on the other hand, a bodily life. When we seem nearest to the vision of God in this life, the body seems almost an irrelevance. And if we try to conceive our eternal life as one in a body (any kind of body) we tend to find that some vague dream of Platonic paradises and gardens of the Hesperides has substituted itself for that mystical approach which we feel (and I think rightly) to be more important. But if that discrepancy were final then it would follow—which is absurd—that God was originally mistaken when He introduced our spirits into the natural order at all. We must conclude that the discrepancy itself is precisely one of the disorders which the New Creation comes to heal. The fact that the body, and locality and locomotion and time, now feel irrelevant to the highest reaches of the spiritual life is (like the fact that we can think of our bodies as "coarse") a *symptom*. Spirit and Nature have quarreled in us; that is our disease. Nothing we can yet do enables us to imagine its complete healing. Some glimpses and faint hints we have: in the Sacraments, in the use made of sensuous imagery by the great poets, in the best instances of sexual love, in our experiences of the earth's beauty. But the full healing is utterly beyond our present conceptions. Mystics have got as far in contemplation of God as the point at which the senses are banished: the further point, at which they will be put back again, has (to the best of my knowledge) been reached by no one. The destiny of redeemed man is not less but more unimaginable than mysticism would lead us to suppose—because it is full of semi-imaginables which we cannot at present admit without destroying its essential character.

I am well aware that this preceding paragraph may seem to many readers unfortunate and to some comic. But that very comedy, as I must repeatedly insist, is the symptom of our estrangement, as spirits, from Nature and our estrangement, as animals, from Spirit. The whole conception of the New Creation involves the belief that this estrangement will be healed. A curious consequence will follow. The archaic type of thought which could not clearly distinguish spiritual "Heaven" from the sky, is from our point of view a confused type of thought. But it also resembles and anticipates a type of thought which will one day be true. That archaic sort of thinking will become simply the correct sort when Nature and Spirit are fully harmonized—when Spirit rides Nature so perfectly that the two together make rather a centaur than a mounted knight. I do not mean necessarily that the blending of Heaven and sky, in particular, will turn out to be specially true, but that that kind of blending will accurately mirror the reality which will then exist. There will be no room to get the finest razor blade of thought in between Spirit and Nature. Every state of affairs in the New Nature will be the perfect expression of a spiritual state and every spiritual state the perfect informing of, and bloom upon, a state of affairs; one with it as the perfume with a flower or the "spirit" of great poetry with its form. There is thus in the history of human thought, as elsewhere, a pattern of death and rebirth. The old, richly imaginative thought which still survives in Plato has to submit to the deathlike, but indispensable, process of logical analysis: nature and spirit, matter and mind, fact and

myth, the literal and the metaphorical, have to be
more and more sharply separated, till at last a purely
mathematical universe and a purely subjective mind
confront one another across an unbridgeable chasm.
But from this descent also, if thought itself is to
survive, there must be reascent, and the Christian
conception provides for it. Those who attain the
glorious resurrection will see the dry bones clothed
again with flesh, the fact and the myth remarried,
the literal and the metaphorical rushing together.

The remark so often made that "Heaven is a state
of mind" bears witness to the wintry and deathlike
phase of this process in which we are now living. The
implication is that if Heaven is a state of mind—or,
more correctly, of the spirit—then it must be only
a state of the spirit, or at least that anything else, if
added to that state of spirit, would be irrelevant. That
is what every great religion *except* Christianity would
say. But Christian teaching by saying that God made
the world and called it good teaches that Nature or
environment cannot be simply irrelevant to spiritual
beatitude in general, however far in one particular
Nature, during the days of her bondage, they may
have drawn apart. By teaching the resurrection of the
body it teaches that Heaven is not merely a state of
the spirit but a state of the body as well: and therefore
a state of Nature as a whole. Christ, it is true, told
His hearers that the Kingdom of Heaven was "within"
or "among" them. But His hearers were not *merely*

in "a state of mind." The planet He had created was beneath their feet, His sun above their heads; blood and lungs and guts were working in the bodies He had invented, photons and sound waves of His devising were blessing them with the sight of His human face and the sound of His voice. We are never *merely* in a state of mind. The prayer and the meditation made in howling wind or quiet sunshine, in morning alacrity or evening resignation, in youth or age, good health or ill, may be equally, but are differently, blessed. Already in this present life we have all seen how God can take up all these seeming irrelevancies into the spiritual fact and cause them to bear no small part in making the blessing of that moment to be the partciular blessing it was—as fire can burn coal and wood equally but a wood fire is different from a coal one. From this factor of environment Christianity does not teach us to desire a total release. We desire, like St. Paul, not to be unclothed but to be reclothed: to find not the formless Everywhere-and-Nowhere but the promised land, that Nature which will be always and perfectly—as present Nature is partially and intermittently—the instrument for that music which will then arise between Christ and us.

And what, you ask, does it matter? Do not such ideas only excite us and distract us from the more immediate and more certain things, the love of God and our neighbors, the bearing of the daily cross? If you find that they so distract you, think of them no more. I most fully allow that it is of more importance for you or me today to refrain from one sneer or to extend one charitable thought to an enemy than to know all that angels and archangels know about the mysteries of the New Creation. I write of these things not because they are the most important but because this book is about miracles. From the title you cannot have expected a book of devotion or of ascetic theology. Yet I will not admit that the things we have been discussing for the last few pages are of no importance for the practice of the Christian life. For I suspect that our conception of Heaven as *merely* a state of mind is not unconnected with the fact that the specifically Christian virtue of Hope has in our time grown so languid. Where our fathers, peering into the future, saw gleams of gold, we see only the mist, white, featureless, cold and never moving.

The thought at the back of all this negative spirituality is really one forbidden to Christians. They, of all men, must not conceive spiritual joy and worth as things that need to be rescued or tenderly protected from time and place and matter and the senses. Their God is the God of corn and oil and wine. He is the glad Creator. He has become Himself incarnate. The sacraments have been instituted. Certain spiritual gifts are offered us only on condition that we perform certain bodily acts. After that we cannot really be in doubt of His intention. To shrink back from all that can be called Nature into negative spirituality is as if we ran away from horses instead of learning to ride. There is in our present pilgrim condition plenty of room (more room than most of us like) for abstinence and renunciation and mortifying our natural desires. But behind all asceticism the thought should be, "Who will trust us with the true wealth if we cannot be trusted even with the wealth that perishes?" Who will trust me with a spiritual body if I cannot control even an earthly body? These small and perishable bodies we now have were given to us as ponies are given to schoolboys. We must learn to manage: not that we may some day be free of horses altogether but that some day we may ride bareback, confident and rejoicing, those greater mounts, those winged, shining and world-shaking horses which perhaps even now expect us with impatience, pawing and snorting in the King's stables. Not that the gallop would be of any value unless it were a gallop with the King; but how else —since He has retained His own charger—should we accompany Him?

Notes by Chapters

CHAPTER I. *The Scope of This Book*

1. Not more "Gods" but other things which God has created but has not interlocked with the system we call Nature: that is, they would have no spatial, temporal, or causal relation at all with the things we know.

CHAPTER III. *Miracle and the Laws of Nature*

1. If any region of reality is in fact chancey or lawless then it is a region which, so far from admitting Miracle with special ease, renders the word "Miracle" meaningless throughout that region.

CHAPTER IV. *"Horrid Red Things"*

1. *Senex mente confusus* Cassian quoted in Gibbon, cap. xlvii.
2. Athanasian Creed.
3. St. Chrysostom *De Incomprehensibili* quoted in Otto, *Idea of the Holy*, Appendix I.
4. Athanasius *De Incarnatione* viii.
5. John 1:1.
6. Colossians 1:17.
7. Colossians 1. Ἐναὐτῷ Ἐκτίσθη John 1:4.
8. Ephesians 10.
9. Jeremiah 23:24.

10. Ezekiel 1:26.
11. Deuteronomy 4:15.
12. Genesis 1:1.

Chapter VI. *On Probability*

1. *Science and the Modern World* by Alfred North Whitehead (New York: The Macmillan Company).

Chapter VIII. *Miracles of the Old Creation*

1. Mark 11:23; 16:17-18. John 14:12.
2. Philippians 3:21. 1 John 3:2.

Chapter IX. *Miracles of the New Creation*

1. That is, the Body with its five senses.